Mel Bay Presents

MW00452329

Fiddler Magazine's Favorites

CD CONTENTS

Disc 1

1	Going To Chattanooga [2:38]
2	Josie Girl [3:28]
3	Oh, Lady Be Good [3:59]
4	Concertina Hornpipe/The Homer Spit [3:36]
5	Jumpin' the Strings [2:37]
6	Long Acre/Clyde's Banks [3:16]
7	Take A Break [3:08]
8	Madame Etienne [2:29]
9	Jackie I Hardly Knew Ya [1:04]
10	Maysville [2:36]
11	Barefoot Fiddler [1:22]
12	Five Miles of Ellum Wood [2:14]
13	Duck River [3:08]
14	The Methodist Preacher [4:09]
15	Fiddler Magazine [2:37]
16	Jim, The Fiddle Maker [3:17]
17	Boo Baby's Lullaby [2:23]
18	Angus MacIsaac's Jig/Alexander William MacDonnell's Jig/John Morris Rankin's Jig [3:04]
19	Bisonpolska [3:30]
20	Lads of Laois/Gan Aimn/The Heathery Cruach [4:41]
21	Limerick's Lamentation [7:15]

Disc 2

1	Road To Silverton [2:44]
2	Big Eddy [3:16]
3	The Sound of Mull/Major Molle's Reel/Miss C. Crawford's Reel [1:52]
4	The Lass of Carrie Mills [1:09]
5	Tommy Don't Go [2:05]
6	Buffalo Girls [2:07]
7	Ninfa [3:58]
8	February Reel #1 [1:48]
9	Horseshoes & Rainbows [3:17]
10	The New Canadian Waltz [3:47]
11	Vallåtspolskan [1:54]
12	Waltz (efter Far) [2:58]
13	Glazier's Hora [2:18]
14	The New House [2:06]
15	The Lovers' Waltz [3:25]
16	La Cadence à Ti-Jules [2:12]
17	Back Home In Indiana [6:07]
18	Forever Young Waltz [2:27]
19	Miss Sarah MacFayden [1:09]

Tunes from and Interviews with 36 of the World's Greatest Fiddlers:

Charlie Acuff • Paul Anastasio • Randal Bays • Byron Berline • Kevin Burke
Vassar Clements • Michael Doucet • Jackie Dunn • J.P. Fraley • Johnny Gimble
Bruce Greene • Richard Greene • John Hartford • Ivan Hicks • Jerry Holland • Olov Johansson
James Kelly • Barbara Lamb • Laurie Lewis • Sandy MacIntyre • Natalie MacMaster
Frankie McWhorter • Bruce Molsky • Juan Reynoso • Dale Russ • Oliver Schroer
Pierre Schryer • Björn Ståbi • Alicia Svigals • Athena Tergis & Laura Risk • Jay Ungar
Jean-Marie Verret • Claude Williams • George Wilson • Jennifer Wrigley

Styles include Old-Time, Bluegrass, Swing, Jazz, Irish, Scottish, Cape Breton, Swedish, Klezmer, Mexican, French Canadian...

Cover photo credit: © Thomas Fahlander

Visit us on the Web at http://www.melbay.com — E-mail us at email@melbay.com

1 2 3 4 5 6 7 8 9 0

CD Contents

DISC ONE:

1. "Going to Chattanooga" — **Charlie Acuff**
(John Hartford, banjo)
Traditional
Source cassette: *Left-Handed Fiddler*
Charlie Acuff, 942 Birch St., Alcoa, TN 37701

2. "Josie Girl" — **Charlie Acuff**
(John Hartford, banjo)
Traditional
Source cassette: *Left-Handed Fiddler*
Charlie Acuff, 942 Birch St., Alcoa, TN 37701

3. "Oh, Lady Be Good" — **Paul Anastasio**
(Jack Hansen, guitar)
Source CD: *Mount Baker Swing* (Swing Cat 1493)
Swing Cat Productions, P.O. Box 30153, Seattle, WA 98103;
(206) 440-1844; panastasio@w-link.net

4. "Concertina Hornpipe"/"The Homer Spit" — **Randal Bays**
"Concertina Hornpipe": Traditional
"The Homer Spit": By Randal Bays
Source CD: *Out of the Woods* (©1997, Foxglove Records FG9701CD)
Foxglove Records, P.O. Box 30083, Seattle, WA 98103;
(206) 706-3230; http://www.teleport.com/~fg/index.html

5. "Jumpin' the Strings" — **Byron Berline**
(Alan Munde, banjo; Dan Crary, guitar; Joe Carr, guitar;
Bill Bryson, bass)
By Byron Berline
Source CD: *Jumpin' the Strings* (©1990, Sugar Hill CD-3787)
Sugar Hill Records, P.O. Box 55300, Durham, NC 27717;
(800) 996-4455; http://www.sugarhillrecords.com

6. "The Long Acre" /"Clyde's Banks" — **Kevin Burke**
(Mark Graham, harmonica; Paul Kotapish, guitar)
By Kevin Burke
Source CD: *Open House* (©1992, Green Linnet Records GLCD 1122)
Green Linnet, 43 Beaver Brook Rd., Danbury, CT 06810;
(800) 468-6644; http://www.greenlinnet.com

7. "Take A Break" — **Vassar Clements**
(Reggie Harris, guitar; Stephen Davidowski, piano; Ray Von Rotz, drums &
percussion; Jim Stephens, bass)
By Vassar and Millie Clements, © Vassar's Music, ASCAP.
Source CD: *Vassar's Jazz, Golden Anniversary Album* CD (©1997 Winter
Harvest WH 3311-2)
Vassillie Productions, (888) 222-9505; http://mbus.com/vassar

8. "Madame Etienne" — **Michael Doucet**
(Charles Sawtelle, guitar)
Traditional
Source CD: *Fiddler Magazine's* 1999 Tune-A-Month Calendar CD

9. "Jackie I Hardly Knew Ya" — **Jackie Dunn**
(Hilda Chiasson-Cormier, piano; David MacIsaac, guitar)
By Jackie Dunn
Source CD: *Dunn To a "T"*
Jackie Dunn, P.O. Box 138, Judique, N.S., Canada B0E 1P0, (902) 787-2117

10. "Maysville" — **J.P. Fraley**
(Annadeene Fraley, guitar; Doug Chaffin, bass)
©Happy Valley Music, Ltd.
Source CD: *J.P. and Annadeene Fraley: Maysville* (©1995 Rounder CD 0351)
Rounder Records, One Camp Street, Cambridge, MA 02140, (800) 44-DISCS;
http://www.rounder.com

11. "Barefoot Fiddler" — **Johnny Gimble**
(Jim Boyd, guitar)
By Johnny Gimble
Source CD: *The Texas Fiddle Collection* (©1989 CMH Records
CD-9027)
CMH Records, Inc., P.O. Box 39439, Los Angeles, CA 90039;
(323) 663-8073

12. "Five Miles of Ellum Wood" — **Bruce Greene**
Traditional
Source CD: *Five Miles of Ellum Wood* (©1997 Bruce Greene)
Bruce Greene, Route 5, Box 340, Burnsville, NC 28714

13. "Duck River" — **Bruce Greene**
Traditional
Source cassette: *Vintage Fiddle Tunes* (©Bruce Greene)
Bruce Greene, Route 5, Box 340, Burnsville, NC 28714

14. "The Methodist Preacher" — **Richard Greene**
(Bill Keith, banjo; David Grier, guitar; Kenny Blackwell, mandolin; Tim
Emmons, bass)
Traditional
Source CD: *The Grass Is Greener* (©1995 Rebel Records
REB-CD-1714)
Rebel Records, P.O. Box 3057, Roanoke, VA 24015

15. "Fiddler Magazine" — **John Hartford**
(Chris Sharp, guitar; Mike Compton, mandolin)
By John Hartford, ©1998 John Hartford Music, BMI
John Hartford Music/Small Dog A-Barkin', P.O. Box 443,
Madison, TN 37116; http://www.techpublishing.com/hartford/

16. "Jim, the Fiddle Maker" — **Ivan Hicks**
By Ivan Hicks
Source cassette: *Friendly Fiddling The Maritime Way*
Ivan Hicks, 157 Sussex Ave., Riverview, New Brunswick, Canada EIB 3A8;
(506) 386-2996; email: hicksi@nb.sympatico.ca

17. "Boo Baby's Lullaby" — **Jerry Holland**
(J.P. Cormier, guitar)
By Jerry Holland
Source CD: *Fiddler's Choice* (©1999 Odyssey Records)
Odyssey Records, 125 South Wacker Dr., Suite 300, Chicago, IL 60606-4402,
(312) 214-2525; http://www.odysseyrecords.com

18. "Angus MacIsaac's Jig"/"Alexander William MacDonnell's
Jig"/"John Morris Rankin's Jig" — **Jerry Holland**
(Ciaran O'Hare, uilleann pipes; Mary Jessie Gillis, piano; Gordie Sampson,
guitar)
By Jerry Holland
Source CD: *Fiddler's Choice* (©1999 Odyssey Records)
Odyssey Records, 125 South Wacker Dr., Suite 300, Chicago, IL 60606-4402,
(312) 214-2525; http://www.odysseyrecords.com

19. "Bisonpolska" — **Olov Johansson**
(Olov Johansson, nyckelharpa; Mikael Marin, viola; Roger Tallroth, guitar)
By Olov Johansson, published by Drone Music AB.
Source CDs: *Vilda Väsen* (©1992 Drone Records DROCD004);
licensed to NorthSide for Väsen's *Spirit* CD (©1997 NorthSide NSD6004)
Drone: http://www.drone.se
NorthSide: 530 North Third St., Minneapolis, MN 55401,
(612) 375-0233; http://www.noside.com

20. "Lads of Laois"/"Gan Aimn"/"The Heathery Cruach"
— **James Kelly**
(Zan McLeod, guitar)
Traditional
Source CD: *James Kelly* (©1997 Capelhouse Records CD896012)
Capelhouse Records, 558 E. Bethel Road, Bethel, ME 04217, (207) 875-
2272.

21. "Limerick's Lamentation" — **James Kelly**
(Zan McLeod, guitar)
Traditional
Source CD: *James Kelly* (©1997 Capelhouse Records CD896012)
Capelhouse Records, 558 E. Bethel Road, Bethel, ME 04217, (207) 875-
2272.

DISC TWO:

1. "Road to Silverton" — **Barbara Lamb**
   (Laura Love, bass)
   By Barbara Lamb and Laura Love
   (Barbara Lamb, Let 'er Buck Music (ASCAP), ©1998)
   Source CD: *Fiddler Magazine's* 1999 Tune-A-Month Calendar CD

2. "Big Eddy" — **Laurie Lewis**
   (Tom Rozum, mandolin; Todd Phillips, bass; Craig Smith, banjo; Mary Gibbons, guitar)
   By Laurie Lewis and Tom Rozum, Spruce and Maple Music (ASCAP). Source CD: *Laurie Lewis and Her Bluegrass Pals* (©1999 Rounder CD 0461)
   Rounder Records, One Camp Street, Cambridge, MA 02140, (800) 44-DISCS; http://www.rounder.com

3. "The Sound of Mull" (Traditional)/"Major Molle's Reel" (Traditional)/"Miss C. Crawford's Reel" (Robert Mackintosh) — **Sandy MacIntyre**
   (Doug MacPhee, piano)
   Source CD: *Island Treasure, vol. 1* (©1998 Sandy MacIntyre Productions SM 9107)
   Sandy MacIntyre Productions,Inc., 1 Aberfoyle Crescent, Suite 1702, Etobicoke, Ontario, Canada M8X 2X8

4. "The Lass of Carrie Mills" — **Natalie MacMaster**
   (Howie MacDonald, piano)
   Traditional
   Source CD: *Fit As A Fiddle* (©1997 Rounder CD 7022/©1993 Warner Music Canada)
   Rounder Records, One Camp Street, Cambridge, MA 02140, (800) 44-DISCS; http://www.rounder.com
   Warner Music Canada, Ltd., 3751 Victoria Park Ave., Scarborough, Ontario, Canada M1W 3Z4; (416) 491-5005; Fax: (416) 491-8203

5. "Tommy Don't Go" — **Frankie McWhorter**
   (Curley Hollingsworth, piano; Tommy Allsup, bass, guitar; Jim Benjamin, drums; Bobby Koefer, steel guitar; Tommy Morrell, Dobro; Larry McWhorter, clarinet)
   Traditional, arranged by Frankie McWhorter
   Source CD: *The Ranch Dance Fiddle: Frankie McWhorter* (©1997 Fiel Publications, Inc. FPRS 0005)
   Fiel Publications, Inc. 3716-27th St., Lubbock,TX 79410, (806) 791-3967; http://www.ranchdance.com

6. "Buffalo Girls" — **Bruce Molsky**
   (Audrey Molsky, guitar)
   Traditional
   Source CD: *Lost Boy* (©1996 Rounder CD 0361)
   Rounder Records, One Camp Street, Cambridge, MA 02140, (800) 44-DISCS; http://www.rounder.com

7. "Ninfa" — **Juan Reynoso**
   (Neyo and Javier Reynoso, guitars)
   ©1998 Juan Reynoso. All rights reserved.
   Source CD: *Viva Tierra Caliente* (Vol. 3 of Swing Cat's Juan Reynoso series)
   Swing Cat, P.O. Box 30153, Seattle, WA 98103; (206) 440-1844
   panastasio@w-link.net; http://www.w-link.net/~panastasio/

8. "February Reel #1" (F#m Reel #1) — **Dale Russ**
   (Mike Saunders, guitar)
   By Dale Russ
   Source CD: Dale Russ, *Irish Fiddle* (Aniar Records) (prev. Foxglove Records ©1995)
   Aniar Records, P.O. Box 210481, San Francisco, CA 94121, (415) 759-8370; http://www.aniar.com

9. "Horseshoes & Rainbows" — **Oliver Schroer**
   (Kelly McGowan, brush bodhran; David Travers Smith, trumpet; David Woodhead, fretless bass)
   By Oliver Schroer
   Source CD: *Jigzup* (©1993 Big Dog Music BD9301CD)
   Big Dog Music, 589 Markham St., Toronto, Ontario, Canada M6G 2L7; (416) 516-4806

10. "The New Canadian Waltz" — **Pierre Schryer**
    (Julie Schryer-Lefebvre, piano)
    By Pierre Schryer, ©1994 SOCAN
    Source CD: *The New Canadian Waltz* (©1996 New Canadian Records NCCD-9610)
    New Canadian Records, P.O. Box 20046, 150 Churchill Blvd., Sault Ste. Marie, Ontario, Canada P6A 6W3; Fax: (705) 246-0252

11. "Vallåtspolskan" — **Björn Ståbi**
    Traditional
    Source CD: *Orsalåtar* (© Giga GCD-35)
    Giga Folkmusik HB, Borsheden, S-780 40 Mockfjärd, Sweden; Phone: (+46-241) 20080; Fax: (+46-241) 21070; giga.folkmusik@giga.w.se; http://www.giga.w.se

12. "Waltz (efter Far)" — **Björn Ståbi**
    Traditional
    Source CD: *Orsalåtar* (© Giga GCD-35)
    Giga Folkmusik HB, Borsheden, S-780 40 Mockfjärd, Sweden; Phone: (+46-241) 20080; Fax: (+46-241) 21070; giga.folkmusik@giga.w.se; http://www.giga.w.se

13. "Glazier's Hora" — **Alicia Svigals**
    (Lauren Brody, accordion)
    By Alicia Svigals
    Source CD: *Fidl* (©1997 Traditional Crossroads CD 4286)
    Traditional Crossroads, P.O. Box 20320 Greeley Sq. Sta., New York, NY 10001-9992; (212) 579-3761; tradcross@aol.com

14. "The New House" — **Athena Tergis and Laura Risk**
    (Steve Baughman, guitar; Pat Klobas, bass; Peter Maund, percussion)
    By Laura Risk
    Source CD: *Journey Begun* (©1994 Culburnie Records CUL 105D-CD/ CUL105C-Cassette).)
    Culburnie Records, P.O. Box 219, Nevada City, CA 95959; (800) 830-6296/ (530) 292-4219; usinfo@culburnie.com; http://www.culburnie.com

15. "The Lovers' Waltz" — **Jay Ungar**
    (Molly Mason, piano)
    By Jay Ungar and Molly Mason, ©1993 Swinging Door Music-BMI
    Source CD: *The Lovers' Waltz* (©1997 Angel Records 7243 5 55561)
    Angel Records, 304 Park Ave. South, New York, NY 10010; (212) 253-3000; http://www.angelrecords.com

16. "La Cadence à Ti-Jules" — **Jean-Marie Verret**
    (Jean-Marie and Martin Verret, fiddle; Lyse Verret, piano)
    SOCAN
    Source CD: *Quadrilles du XIXe et XXe siècle* (©1997 Thirty Below TB-134-CD)
    Thirty Below, 1108 rue Dollard, Val-Bélair, Québec, Canada G3K 1W6; Phone & Fax: (418) 847-9815; thirtybe@qbc.clic.net; http://www.qbc.clic.net/~thirtybe

17. "Back Home In Indiana" — **Claude Williams**
    (James Chirillo, guitar; Ron Mathews, piano; Akira Tana, drums; Al McKibbon, bass)
    Source CD: *Live At J's, Volume 2* (©1993 Arhoolie CD 406)
    Arhoolie Productions, Inc., 10341 San Pablo Ave., El Cerrito, CA 94530. Toll-free: 888-ARHOOLIE. http://www.arhoolie.com
    Also available: CD 405: *Live At J's, Volume 1*.

18. "Forever Young Waltz" — **George Wilson**
    By George Wilson
    (George Wilson: fiddle & guitar)
    George Wilson, 10 Loomis Road, Wynantskill, NY 12198; (518) 283-4957.

19. "Miss Sarah MacFayden" — **Jennifer Wrigley**
    (Hazel Wrigley, piano and guitar)
    By Jennifer Wrigley
    Source CD: *The Watch Stone* (©1994 Attic Records ATCD038)
    Attic Records, Keldabrae, Finstown, Orkney Isles; Phone: (01856) 761222

We hope you'll enjoy this book and CD set, and we offer our sincere thanks to Bill Bay of Mel Bay Publications for taking on the project, and to all of the wonderful fiddlers for sharing their music. In addition to the 46 tunes in this book, you'll find excerpts from interviews and articles from the first five years of *Fiddler Magazine*; this way, you'll be able to get to know the fiddlers whose music you'll be listening to and playing. The musicians and record companies involved have generously given their permission to include these tunes, so please be sure to seek out the source recordings for any of the tunes you especially like.

If you're not familiar with *Fiddler Magazine,* please see the subscription form at the back of the book for more information.

Thank you for purchasing this collection. Now, put on that CD, get out your fiddle, and have fun!

Mary Larsen, Editor, *Fiddler Magazine*

Jack Tuttle, Music Editor, *Fiddler Magazine*

Notation in Finale by Jack Tuttle.

About the Authors:

Peter Anick, co-editor of Mel Bay's *Old-Time Fiddling Across America,* plays fiddle and guitar in the Massachusetts-based bluegrass band Waystation.

Guy Bouchard is co-owner (with his wife Laura Sadowsky) of Thirty Below (Trente sous zéro), a mail-order business offering Québécois recordings, books, and videos: http://www.qbc.clic.net/~thirtybe.

Bob Buckingham of Pennsylvania is a fiddler, old time banjo player, and leader of the Contra Rebels, an old time stringband. He is on the writing staff of *Bluegrass Unlimited* and *Fiddler Magazine* and is a frequent contributor to *The Old Time Herald* and *The Devil's Box.*

Susan Conger lives in western Massachusetts, where she teaches fiddle, plays for contra and Swedish dances, and writes tunes. She has recorded with the bands Three Good Reasons and Spare Parts. She is currently compiling a book of tunes by Connecticut River Valley composers.

Jim D'Ville is the host of the bluegrass and old-time radio show String Time Serenade on KORC AM 820, Waldport, Oregon.

Lindajoy Fenley is the founder and director of Dos Tradiciones, A.C., a non-profit organization to foster cultural exchange between Mexico and other countries. She also hosts a short wave radio show about Mexican music and culture called "Regional Roots and Rhythms" on Radio Mexico International (XERMX.OC: 31 mts. 9705 kHz and 49 mts. 5985 kHz).

Matt Fichtenbaum of Massachusetts has taught nyckelharpa in both the U.S. and Sweden. He plays Scandinavian fiddle and contradance fiddle and piano for dancing in the Boston area.

Lanny Fiel is a Texas musician and producer twice recognized with the Western Heritage Wrangler Award from the National Cowboy Hall of Fame. He works with cowboy fiddler Frankie McWhorter and other artists to document traditions of the Texas Plains.

Patrice George is a founding member of the New York Spelmanslag, a group of fiddlers who play for Scandinavian dances. She has been a contributing writer for *Fiddler Magazine* since 1995.

Larry Hill has played Irish music on fiddle, flute, and whistle for twenty years.

Niles Hokkanen plays mandolin, drums and jouhikko, and plays with the Finnish band Nordika. He writes for various music magazines, and has instructional materials available for the mandolin (P.O. Box 3585, Winchester, VA 22604).

Paul Jacobs plays mandolin, guitar, and fiddle, and is a founding member of the bands Earthquake Country, The Tarnation Band, and The Love Slaves. He hosts weekly bluegrass and blues radio shows on KKUP FM 91.5, Cupertino, California.

Mary Larsen, Editor and Publisher of *Fiddler Magazine,* enjoys listening to all styles of fiddle music. She founded *Fiddler Magazine* upon her return from a trip to Ireland in 1993, where she attended the Willie Clancy summer school in County Clare.

Donna Maurer is currently playing traditional Irish fiddle in sessions in Colorado Springs. She also plays other styles and instruments, including rock on an electric 5-string violin.

Hollis Payer is an actor, writer, and musician living in Philadelphia. She's been studying and playing traditional Irish music on the fiddle since first hearing it during her travels in Ireland in the early '80s. She is currently at work on an audio documentary exploring traditional music in North America.

Jack Tuttle, *Fiddler Magazine*'s Music Editor, has been a professional fiddle player and instructor for twenty years, and has performed in the U.S., Canada and Japan. He has been a member of numerous bands, including the Gryphon Quintet (swing) and Emerald (Celtic), and currently plays with the Tall Timber Boys (bluegrass). Jack has taught over a thousand students to play banjo, mandolin, guitar and fiddle in both private and group lessons, as well as at the Festival of American Fiddle Tunes and the California Coast Music Camp.

Charlie "Possum" Walden is president of the Missouri State Old-Time Fiddlers' Association, as well as a first rate fiddler and champion of regional fiddle styles. His recordings include *Draggin' the Bow, Traditional Fiddle, Poss Trax,* and *Patt and Possum.*

Book Contents

Fiddlers		Tunes	
Charlie Acuff	6	"Going to Chattanooga"	8
		"Josie Girl"	8
Paul Anastasio	9	"Oh, Lady Be Good!"	10
Randal Bays	13	"The Concertina Hornpipe"	15
		"The Homer Spit" (hornpipe)	15
Byron Berline	16	"Jumpin' the Strings"	18
Kevin Burke	19	"The Long Acre"	21
		"Clyde's Banks"	21
Vassar Clements	22	"Take a Break"	25
Michael Doucet	26	"Madame Etienne"	29
Jackie Dunn	30	"Jackie I Hardly Knew Ya"	31
J.P. Fraley	32	"Maysville"	34
Johnny Gimble	35	"Barefoot Fiddler"	37
Bruce Greene	38	"Five Miles of Ellum Wood"	40
		"Duck River"	40
Richard Greene	41	"The Methodist Preacher"	44
John Hartford	45	"Fiddler Magazine"	48
Ivan Hicks	49	"Jim, the Fiddle Maker"	50
Jerry Holland	51	"Boo Baby's Lullaby"	52
		"Angus MacIsaac's Jig"	52
		"Alexander William MacDonnell's Jig"	53
		"John Morris Rankin's Jig"	53
Olov Johansson	55	"Bisonpolska"	57
James Kelly	58	"The Lads of Laois"	60
		"Limerick's Lamentation"	61
Barbara Lamb	62	"Road to Silverton"	64
Laurie Lewis	65	"Big Eddy"	67
Sandy MacIntyre	68	"The Sound of Mull"	68
		"Major Molle's Reel"	69
		"Miss C. Crawford's Reel"	69
Natalie MacMaster	71	"The Lass of Carrie Mills"	72
Frankie McWhorter	73	"Tommy Don't Go"	74
Bruce Molsky	76	"Buffalo Girls"	78
Juan Reynoso	79	"Ninfa"	81
Dale Russ	82	"February Reel #1"	84
Oliver Schroer	85	"Horseshoes & Rainbows"	86
Pierre Schryer	87	"The New Canadian Waltz"	89
Björn Ståbi	90	"Vallåtspolskan"	91
		"Waltz (efter Far)"	92
Alicia Svigals	93	"Glazier's Hora"	95
Athena Tergis & Laura Risk	96	"The New House"	98
Jay Ungar	99	"The Lovers' Waltz"	101
Jean-Marie Verret	102	"La Cadence à Ti-Jules"	104
Claude "Fiddler" Williams	105	"Back Home In Indiana"	106
George Wilson	109	"Forever Young Waltz"	111
Jennifer & Hazel Wrigley	112	"Miss Sarah MacFayden"	114

A Chat with Charlie Acuff: East Tennessee Fiddler

By Mary Larsen

Charlie at the Museum of Appalachia, 1997

Charlie Acuff was born in Maynardville, eastern Tennessee, in 1919. Cousin of the late Roy Acuff, Charlie says with a chuckle, "All of us Acuffs were musicians, but Roy's the one that made the money!"

Charlie learned to play the fiddle from his grandfather, Charles B. Acuff, when he was about twelve years old. He was soon playing in bands in high school for square dances, and on radio station WROL in Knoxville. After graduating from high school, Charlie went to work for the Aluminum Company of America in Alcoa, from which he retired in 1982. Throughout his working years, Charlie continued to play his fiddle. Today he performs regularly with the popular Lantana Drifters, and plays once a week, April through December, at the Museum of Appalachia in Norris, Tennessee, as well as at the Museum's Tennessee Fall Homecoming every October.

Charlie is both a fine old time fiddler and a delightful and gracious person. I had the privilege of taking workshops from him at the 1994 Festival of American Fiddle Tunes in Port Townsend, Washington, where he was accompanied by folklorist Bobby Fulcher on banjo and guitar. ["Fiddle Tunes was one of the highlights of my life," says Charlie.] I talked with him again at the Museum of Appalachia the following October, where he was playing his fiddle off and on from nine in the morning until nearly seven in the evening for four days. "You'll need a vacation after this weekend, Charlie," I said on the last day of the festival. "Well, I've got two days off, then I'll be back on Wednesday." A fiddler to the core!

Did your grandfather give you lessons, or did you learn more by watching him and listening to him?

He pasted a piece of paper on the fingerboard to show me where to put the fingers, and then he showed me which finger goes where. And I would learn the tunes in sections — maybe I'd first learn about three or four notes, and he'd have me play them over and over, and after I played them, he'd add a little more to it, and then I'd have a tune, you see.

How did you decide to play left-handed? Did you think about it?

Well, I was staying with my grandfather, and he asked me did I ever get my daddy's fiddle down and play, and I told him, no, I was left-handed. And he said, "Well, we'll just see about that." He had known other left-handed fiddlers, you know. I guess I've known probably fifteen or eighteen.

Do you think it's more difficult than playing right-handed?

Well, some things are more difficult to play, while with others, it's kind of handy for me.

Where did your grandfather learn to play the fiddle?

He learned different places. His uncle Gordon — they called him Uncle Gord Cassady — played, and he learned several tunes from him. And his uncle Fate Cassidy… He was in the Civil War and he was a blacksmith. He made the tools to make fiddles with, and whenever he got old, why he told my daddy, "If you learn to make fiddles, I'll give you my tools, on the condition that you never sell them…"

Do you play mostly your grandfather's tunes, the way he played them?

What I learned from him, I play just like he played them. Now my daddy [Evart Acuff] played, but I didn't learn much from my daddy. He was more interested in making fiddles. But he played this sweet music, a long bow kind of like Ralph Blizard. He didn't play too many tunes. I've got a little different shuffle of the bow than my daddy had.

"[My grandfather] asked me did I ever get my daddy's fiddle down and play, and I told him, no, I was left-handed. And he said, 'Well, we'll just see about that.'"

Can you describe your shuffle?

My grandfather taught me that shuffle. It's just a little more wrist movement. Like these Irish jigs — it's hard for me to play them if I don't shuffle my bow....

Did you play for dances when you were young?

Yeah, I played for square dances. There was just one high school in the county, and me and my brother Gale, and the two Keck boys — H.T. Keck and Glen Keck — Glen played the mandolin and H.T. picked the guitar, and we played for dances. Nearly everything that they had, like the F.F.A. (Future Farmers of America) and the Home Ec Banquet. We got a spot on WROL Radio in Knoxville in 1938. Esco Hankins and his cousin, Bill Guy, came up there to Maynardville where I lived and got me and my brother, and we got a spot up there on WROL. And we played on that station for, I guess, six months, then we had to quit because I was a sophomore in high school — we had to get up about four o'clock, and we were out late at night at times. I couldn't hardly stay awake in school. We booked a few shows — I think we were charging 15¢ and 25¢.

Who did you listen to when you were young? Who were your favorite fiddlers?

Fiddlin' Arthur Smith from Nashville, you know. And after I got a little older and Roy Acuff had Howdy Forester, I enjoyed his fiddling.

Do you still practice?

Yeah. The way I practice is learning new tunes. I hardly ever sit down at something I can already play — I hardly ever practice on it unless I'm with somebody. When I learn a tune I just take a tape and listen to it. Years ago, when I learned, we had no tapes to listen to. You'd have to get with somebody and watch their fingers and listen to them.

Do you have any advice for people interested in learning old time fiddle?

The art of playing the fiddle is in the bow. When I was up at Port Townsend [at the Festival of American Fiddle Tunes in 1994], I stressed that. To make the shuffles of the bow like I do, you've got to have a limber wrist. Some people can play good with a stiff wrist. I never could — or a tight bow. I play with a loose bow and a limber wrist, you know.

Tell me about your fiddle.

I've got five that my daddy made. He made thirty-six. The one I had at Fiddle Tunes was number 33, made in 1969. They're all good fiddles, but they're all different. Number 5 was the one I really learned on, and it was my favorite just about. I wanted him to make one that sounded like his, because he got better on the finishing of them, you know. But you can take a piece of wood, and you can't tell what kind of a tone you're going to get out of it. I had one made like I wanted it to look. I thought it would sound better than anything. It's a good fiddle, but it's not as good as number 33!

How long have you been playing with the Lantana Drifters?

I met them at the Museum of Appalachia and I started playing with them in 1989. They like competitions — we played all down through middle Tennessee at the festivals, and we've won five times in Smithville [Tennessee], five years. We won in '89 and '90, and then we weren't eligible in '91, and in '92 and '93 we won; in '94 we weren't eligible, and I went to the state of Washington then, and in '95 we won again.

For best old time band?

Yeah, old time band, first place.

Since this interview, Charlie hasn't let up a bit. He taught and performed at the Festival of American Fiddle Tunes (Port Townsend, Washington) again in 1996, continues to perform at the Museum of Appalachia, and still plays regularly with the Lantana Drifters. In 1998, he made a highly recommended video for Cedar Glade Productions. He has plans for another recording in 1999.

Discography

- *Left-Handed Fiddler*, with John Hartford (banjo)
- *Mule Skinner Blues,* The Lantana Drifters
- *Wreck of 97,* The Lantana Drifters

Videos:

- *Charlie Acuff, East Tennessee Fiddler* (with Tom Jackson and Andy Smith). Cedar Glade Productions 001. (Available from Charlie Acuff; see address at right.)
- *Carrying on the Traditions: Appalachian Fiddling Today* (Fiddler Magazine FMV-01)

[For bookings or information on his recordings and videos, write to Charlie at 942 Birch St., Alcoa, TN 37701.]

Going to Chattanooga

Transcribed by Jack Tuttle as played by Charlie Acuff on *Left-Handed Fiddler.* Charlie learned these two tunes from his grandfather, Charles B. Acuff.

Lyrics: "If I get drunk and keep it up, I'm going to Chattanooga."

Josie Girl

Transcribed by Jack Tuttle as played by Charlie Acuff on *Left-Handed Fiddler.*

Lyrics: "Where's that girl, where's she gone? Where's the girl with the josie on? Stole my heart, and now she's gone. Where's the girl with the josie on?" [A josie is an overcoat.]

Paul Anastasio: Got That Swing!

By Jack Tuttle

Though it's been twenty years since Paul Anastasio was first cast under the spell of jazz greats Stéphane Grappelli and Joe Venuti, spend any time with him and you'll quickly realize there has been no fading of the passion. Classically trained as a youngster, Anastasio has been relentless in his pursuit of swing/jazz improvising for all of his adult life. Perhaps best known for his playing in the early '80s with the western swing band Asleep At The Wheel, he has also served lengthy stints as fiddle sideman for Merle Haggard, Larry Gatlin and Loretta Lynn.

Having tired of living on the road, Anastasio returned to his native Seattle area roots in 1992, and in addition to performing around town, he has become involved in teaching swing to other aspiring fiddlers. He has made numerous solo recordings — all of them swing oriented, and has an instructional video, "Swing Fiddle," on Ridge Runner. He is currently developing teaching materials that focus on theory and improvising.

It seems like your heart was always in swing.

Yeah, I was drawn to that, and even before I met Venuti, I was able to follow Grappelli around a lot. I followed Stéphane Grappelli around three separate tours of the west coast. I remember seeing him in Vancouver, B.C., and went home and went to sleep and woke up about three hours later with that stuff going through my head, and I knew they were going to play in Los Angeles. And I didn't have a job, I was free to go and do some stuff, so I just took off, drove to L.A.... I remember one time, I had a Volkswagen bus with a transmission leak, so I drove all the way to L.A., and every 150 miles I had to stop and crawl underneath and put transmission fluid in it with a little pump. When I got down there I must have looked like a mechanic on a bad day. And the guys in Grappelli's band let me go and clean up in their room. That was when Grappelli was carrying Diz Dizly, Ike Isaacs and Brian Torpel — it was a great band. I followed them around, so I was very much into that. But I didn't learn solos.

Was there some point when you started studying theory a little bit to help you improvise?

Well, in junior high and high school I was playing in the orchestra, and I continued to study privately. Even when I was playing the swing stuff, I was still taking lessons. And I did three years as a music major at Western Washington University — in Bellingham. But two years as a music major was hard core. You didn't have time to turn around — you were doing the string quartet, you were doing theory, you were doing history, and orchestra, you had your private lessons. It was a heavy course load. I did two years and then I dropped out for a year, and then I started listening more to swing stuff, realizing that people like Venuti and Grappelli had these incredible chops and had a lot of theory. So I went back and did another year....

So when you started college, you knew you wanted to be a swing player?

Well, I wanted to play music, and I was trying a lot of different stuff. I remember being in the practice room and instead of playing what I was supposed to play, I'd take a tune like "Turkey in the Straw," something simple, something accessible, and try to play it in as many different styles as I could. Try to do a Cajun feel on it, or try to do a country Ray Price, Tommy Jackson feel, or a swing feel, or try to do a western swing, or try to do it like a fiddle tune — I'd try to do it as many ways as I could. I was just intrigued by trying to figure out what made a style a style.

So it wasn't so much swing. Plus, at that time, [swing] was considered the outest of the out. You think back at that era twenty years ago, twenty-five years ago, rock and roll was king, commercial country was commercial country, pretty cookie cutter stuff. The jazz that was going on, the hip stuff, was fusion, Chick Corea, Stanley Clarke, all that kind of stuff... The way I look at it is, in the last few years, swing has kind of turned into timeless great art, whereas twenty years ago it was thought of as the squarest thing, "That's Mom and Dad's music," or "It's Grandpa's music," "It's Lawrence Welk," "It's Guy Lombardo." It's so square, and the hip stuff is this new mixture of jazz and rock, the fusion stuff. But what's happened now is that because the music is old enough, it's kind of slipped the generational thing, where it's out one generation and in the next. And now if you say, "Oh, I play classic jazz, I do Duke Ellington and George Gershwin," it's kind of almost accorded the same respect that classical music is. No one really worries about when it was written, or in what generation it was popular.... *(Text continued on page 12.)*

Oh, Lady Be Good!

Stylized melody and hot chorus as played by Paul Anastasio on the *Mount Baker Swing* cassette (Swing Cat Recordings 1493)

Notes on the transcription: A line slanting up into a note indicates a slide (usually from a half or a whole step below the note) up into the note. Similarly, a slanting line following a note indicates a slide down from that note. I've notated the tune as accurately as possible, but I'm not entirely sure exactly how I bowed it. A note in parentheses is a "ghost note" (played very softly or only implied).

— *Paul Anastasio*

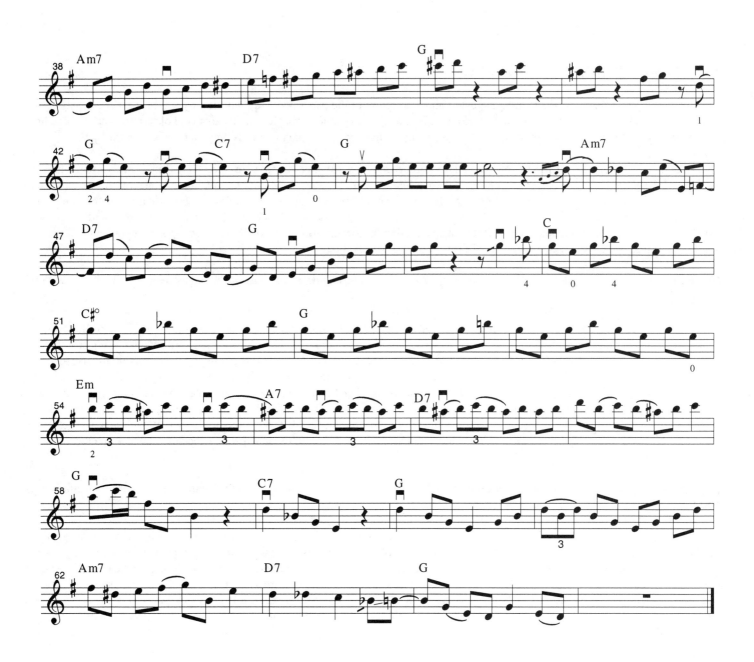

"...In the last few years, swing has kind of turned into timeless great art, whereas twenty years ago it was thought of as the squarest thing, 'That's Mom and Dad's music,' or 'It's Grandpa's music,' 'It's Lawrence Welk,' 'It's Guy Lombardo.'"

At some point did you connect up with Joe Venuti?

Yeah, that was pretty neat....I was reading the entertainment section of the paper and I saw a little tiny squib, Joe Venuti, playing six nights a week for three weeks at a place called the Pioneer Banque, a funky little...what he would call an upholstered sewer. It was a little dive, a basement of a building. I went down, walked in, sat in the front row, and had my mind completely blown by this guy....

Finally, at the end of the run, I just summoned up all my courage and asked Joe for lessons. He said, "Sure, kid, come out to the house." He had me bring the book of Kreutzer Etudes. I had the Joe Venuti book, *The Rhythm Violin Method,* but for some reason, he didn't like that book. I think it's the greatest... He didn't say much about the book, but it's a great introduction to swing rhythm. He told me to play Kreutzer, Bach, and Paganini, in that order. He said, "Don't practice jazz, practice classical. All of jazz is in Bach." And of course, I didn't take his advice at all, I practiced jazz. But then again, I didn't grow up surrounded by it. He grew up in that era, and that was the music, it was like the air that was around you all the time. I had to seek it out.

How have you sought it out in terms of your improvising? Do you rely a lot on instinct and just run through tunes, or do you think in chord tones?

No, I use a system they use in Nashville, which is basically a simplified version of the figured bass, which was in use in Bach's time, where the chords are numbered. Like in a blues tune, there are four bars of one, and two bars of the four chord. When I hear a progression, that's how I'm thinking... I'm building around the chords of the tune, the numbers of the tune, going by what Joe told me. He said you improvise around the basic chords of the tune, which I took to mean you don't necessarily have to acknowledge every little passing movement that's going on, like with a guitar. My whole theory is based on [the notion that] either a note is a chord tone (it's in the chord that's being played at the time) or it's not. If it's not, the ear wants to hear some sort of an explanation, a resolution. The ear has to have a certain amount of dissonance, or else it's going to sound very, very boring. The listener wants to know that you know where you're going with it. So I'm selecting my notes thinking in terms of the numbers of the chords, and also how the notes are numbered in the scale of that chord....

I incorporated some bowing things that I got from Joe... There's a lot of off-beat bowing, from the "and," like "one-**and**-two-**and**-three-**and**-four," across the beat. And you hear that in this old time stuff, too. They'll set up a pattern and they'll break it. I'm listening to it with new ears. Having played bluegrass and old time fiddle tunes and Texas fiddle, kind of running blind on instinct, I'm now going back with greater knowledge. I hear with bigger ears, with more expanded ears, and I start to see that this stuff is a lot more similar than it is different. And what differentiates Cajun style from southeastern old time from Texas old time, western swing, whatever, to a large extent is a matter of nuance, and fine tuning. Like a bebop tune is going to have a lot more neighboring tones and dissonances than a fiddle breakdown... There aren't any wrong notes. There are ways that you can use them that are pleasing to the listener, and there are ways that you can use them that aren't pleasing... Benny Thomasson quotes one of the other Texas fiddle guys as saying that western swing is a matter of fiddling yourself into a hole and then fiddling yourself back out. The ear wants to be surprised, but it wants to hear kind of a happy ending... I want the listeners to have shiny pants, sliding up to the edge of their seat, like "What's he going to do?" And then sliding back in relief when the pattern is resolved.

Partial discography

- *Twin Fiddle Western Swing* (with Dick Barrett) (Swing Cat 1505)
- *Swingin' in Seattle...Live!* (Swing Cat 1504)
- *Spaghetti Rag* (Swing Cat 1500)
- *Serious Swing Jam* (with Ray Wood, guitar) (Swing Cat 1496)
- *Mount Baker Swing* (with Jack Hansen, guitar) (Swing Cat 1493)
- *Swing Time* (with Ken Olendorf, accordion) (Swing Cat 1499)
- *Zombies of Swing* (Swing Cat 1495)
- *The Weiser Workshops, Vol. 1, 2, 3* (cass. only, Swing Cat 1501, 1502, 1503)
- *We Ain't Misbehavin'* (with Joe Holley and Frank Hicks) (LP only, Arhoolie 5032)
- *Paul Anastasio's Folklife Improvisation Workshop* (cass. only, Swing Cat 1498)
- *Paul Anastasio's Swing Instructional Video* (Ridgerunner PA-60)

To order recordings, or for information about bookings or lessons (Paul offers fiddle lessons by the hour, the day, or the week), contact Paul at P.O. Box 30153, Seattle, WA 98103; (206) 782-3282; panastasio@w-link.net; http://www.w-link.net/~panastasio/

Irish Fiddler Randal Bays: An Authenticity of Spirit

By Larry Hill

Photo: Rosalie Borda

Randal Bays comes at you like a summer squall: a little anticipation and suddenly you're drenched. He leads you through a complex musical experience: frolicsome, introspective, lamenting, and plain break-neck fun, and he leaves you with a sense of stimulated well-being. Widely known as the superb guitar accompanist on Martin Hayes' 1993 debut album, Randal first embraced the Irish fiddle more than twenty years ago, devoting both personal and professional focus to the intricacies and subtle nuances of this tradition. With the winter 1997/98 release of his own album, Out of the Woods, he placed himself clearly among the best Irish fiddlers of his generation. He teaches and performs full-time, both here and abroad. He produces recordings for his own label, Foxglove. Witty and engaging, he seeks the smaller stage and the more intimate setting, where performer, music, and audience merge.

You are a traditional musician, and you write new tunes in the tradition. Is there a conflict?

The Irish tradition is a living tradition, unlike some of those that died out and got revived. Irish music never died out. It continued to be a rural peoples' music right up into the present. I mean we're seeing the end of it now, unfortunately. So it has always been a living music, which means it has always been added to. What I've tried to do is to make tunes that sound as though they have the right sense about them. And you can't get too fat a head about it because if you're successful you'll have to come up with tunes that are original and yet have a lot of elements of other things in them that have already gone down. It just seems unnatural not to be making new tunes into a tradition.

You are a professional musician, but do you have a larger purpose?

When I quit the classical guitar, part of it was turning against that whole world of professionalism. I came to not like that paradigm of the performer being separate. You spend all your time: practice, practice, practice. You go up on stage at a huge distance from the audience — put the music out. It's like spectator sports. I'm much more into sandlot softball. Well, I do go to Mariners games.

Everywhere I go, I find a great group of people who are really interested in traditional music on a grass roots level. I play for those people. I find it's the same in Ireland. You have the really big gigs and the fame, but there is this kind of kitchen and small gig oriented thing of people who really appreciate the art of the music. And there's more to it. It's making a connection with people. I travel around this country, and every community harbors people who will come to a house concert. You look out, and the room is full of people who play themselves. So there is generally some element of tune swapping and chatting. Often you're invited to a session with local people when you finish playing. You stay in people's houses. It seems sustainable…. When the trad music is going down someplace, and it's a good scene —like in somebody's house, a late-night session or a concert — the audience is important, they're encouraging, they say things, they show you that they're listening, that they appreciate the things you're doing. It means all the world.

How about some teacher's tips?

It occurred to me that Irish music is like pointillism in painting. Up close, you see a bunch of little dots. You stand back, and there is a beautiful composition. Irish music is a whole lot of little bitty notes. You never dwell on anything longer than an eighth note, usually, but the great players take those little notes, step back from them mentally, and turn them into a lyrical phrase. That's what we're all so drawn to. It is so hard to recreate it when we get hung up on all these individual notes. You have to go through all these stages of technique development to get there. You want to make music, you want to be able to step back and have all those little notes amount to a phrase as beautiful as anything Beethoven wrote. That's the big challenge. Listen to Sean Ryan, or Paddy Fahey.

What can you tell us about the bow?

The connection between the bow and the string — my entire mood, my entire feeling whether my life is going well is totally bound up with whether my bow and my string are working together. The paradoxical right place to be with the bow is completely loose and flexible, but you have total control over it. What happens, when you move forward in your technique with the bow, it feels like you're losing control, and sometimes your ability to play moves backwards for a while. You have to gradually incorporate the increased flexibility to where you have the control to go with it.

*"No matter how much of a beginner you are, what you are playing
is expressing who you are to the world."*

Any advice on repertoire building?

Do it. It is important to learn a standard session repertoire that you can play with people all over the world. People are often attracted to weird tunes, which is great, but nobody can play them with you. A lot of those ceili band albums — Kilfenora Ceili Band, Tulla Ceili Band — those are standards. The recordings of Michael Coleman, James Morrison, Paddy Killoran — everybody needs to hear those, play those. Kevin Burke's recordings, a lot of his material has passed into the realm of standards. Being around and learning from sessions is good. Getting it into your head is the real challenge. It needs to be as familiar as Beatles songs. When it is that familiar, it is going to come out sounding right.

Tell me about Foxglove Records.

It's a very low key thing. I made an album. It wasn't accepted by either of the two big East coast labels, so I decided I'd just make up a label. Then Dale Russ made an album, and we put it on the label. Same with the Suffering Gaels. Then Joel Bernstein and I as the Rashers. Then Jody's Heaven. It never was intended to turn into anything like a big business. I don't have the time or energy. I'm too busy making music and I don't want that to change. I don't want to be a business man sitting around selling albums. So, it's possible other people will get involved and turn it into a business, or it could stay a very minor thing.

What this has done for those of us in the Northwest — we've all been playing for a long time, and the quality of what we do is right up there with anybody else — this has given us a chance to have a little credibility, visibility. Maybe it will mean that some of the people on the label will be able to move on to a higher level of recognition. But I don't expect Foxglove to ever become any kind of corporate entity.

By way of closure, can you reflect a bit?

When I got into this I had no attraction on an ethnic interest level. The music itself is what attracted me. I see so many people who are so passionate about it, so I ask myself, why is it? I find over the years, the dynamics of how this music works — the music itself, the performance settings, the scene — it has a lot in common with blues or jazz. It is a social music, an intense music, and it's a music that respects and honors wildness. That's really important. It's not necessarily always a nice music. In fact, that's another place where us Yanks get into trouble with it. We want everything to be democratic and nice. This music isn't that way. Sometimes it's wild and intense and fiery.

I'd like to say here: we need to take this music seriously. Somewhere else put: we really shouldn't take this music too seriously. Both are true. I go into these sessions and see people staring intensely at the floor, I want to say, "Lighten up. Joke with the person next to you. Have some fun." On the other hand — take it seriously because it's a precious heritage, whether you're Irish or not.

When you play music, regardless of your technical level, the music that comes out is who you are. So, as you go into this stuff, years go by, you're refining your musical expression, but it's becoming more and more who you are. It is kind of like your character, your personality, gets into it and becomes part of the process. It's important to keep that in mind from the beginning. No matter how much of a beginner you are, what you are playing is expressing who you are to the world. You can't hope it's going to be anything other than that. It's just the way it is. Anyway, it's fun.

Partial Discography

- *Out of the Woods,* 1997, solo album (Foxglove Records)
- *Pigtown Fling,* 1996, with Joel Bernstein (Foxglove Records)
- *Wind on the Water,* Nancy Curtin & the Strayaways, 1995 (Foxglove)
- *Under the Moon,* 1995, with Martin Hayes (Green Linnet)
- *John Williams,* 1995, with John Williams (Green Linnet)

- *Martin Hayes,* 1993, with Martin Hayes (Green Linnet)
- *The Traveller's Return,* 1990, with Nancy Curtin
- *The Rashers,* 1988, with Joel Bernstein
- *Nancy Curtin,* 1985, with Nancy Curtin
- *Celtic Music of the Northwest,* 1982, with Wildgeese

Other Foxglove Recordings:
- *Ways of the World,* Ruthie Dornfeld, Joel Bernstein, Keith Murphy, 1998

- *Jody's Heaven,* Dale Russ, Jack Gilder, Junji Shirota, 1997
- *The One-Horned Cow,* The Suffering Gaels, 1996
- *Irish Fiddle,* Dale Russ, 1995

Information on gigs, lessons, or recordings: (206) 706-3230; Fax: (206) 789-6301; Email: fg@teleport.com; Website: http:// www.teleport.com/~fg/index.html

The Concertina Hornpipe

Traditional. Transcribed by Randal Bays as played on his *Out of the Woods* CD (Foxglove FG9701CD).

*"In France I met with a number of excellent players of Irish traditional music. Among the finest were fiddler
Vincent Blin and box player Gilles Poutoux, whose CD 'More Power to Your Elbow' was the source for 'The Concertina
Hornpipe,' which can be found in 'O'Neill's Music of Ireland' as 'The Bath Road Hornpipe.' — Randal Bays*

The Homer Spit (hornpipe)

By Randal Bays, from his *Out of the Woods* CD (Foxglove FG9701CD).

*"The Homer Spit is named for a small piece of land that sticks out into Kachemak Bay at Homer, Alaska.
I've played a lot in Alaska and love the place and the people." — Randal Bays*

Byron Berline:
Gracing the Strings

By Paul Jacobs

For more than thirty years, Byron Berline's graceful fiddle playing has been featured on dozens of recordings by artists as diverse as Bill Monroe, The Dillards, the Rolling Stones, the Flying Burrito Brothers, Country Gazette, and Henry Mancini. Born in Caldwell, Kansas, and raised in Oklahoma, Byron was influenced early on by his father, Lue Berline, a championship old time fiddler, to take up the fiddle and make a career in music. Along the way, Byron became a highly sought-after session player and a triple-threat instrumentalist (fiddle, guitar and mandolin).

After spending twenty-six years in California, Byron is now living in Guthrie, Oklahoma, operating Byron's Double Stop Music Shop and Music Hall, selling instruments, custom videos, putting on shows, and running an annual international bluegrass festival. His new recording with the Byron Berline Band, Live at the Music Hall, *is a mix of traditional fiddle tunes, bluegrass and swing. The band can also be heard every Saturday night on radio shows out of Witchita, Kansas (KFDI),and Tulsa, Oklahoma (KVOO).*

You started playing the fiddle when you were five years old — did you keep up all through your youth and adolescence?

Oh, yeah, sure. My dad would take me to contests all around, mainly in Oklahoma, and he kept talking about these Texas fiddlers he remembered, like Major Franklin — he knew him. Of course he liked Howdy Forrester — we used to listen to [him on] the Grand Ol' Opry. He liked Arthur Smith's fiddle playing. But we finally got to go to a contest back in New Mexico when I was about sixteen years old. And a lot of the Texas fiddlers were there. We went to Hale Center, Texas, which is down by Plainview, Texas, and that's where I got to meet all the Texas type fiddlers — The Solomons, The Franklins, and Benny Thomasson, Eck Robertson. It was great to be able to hear those types of fiddlers when I was fifteen or sixteen years old, and that kind of changed my whole outlook. My dad played almost that style but didn't improvise as much. He was a little more straight-ahead fiddler. But then the only albums you could listen to back when I was growing up were Tommy Jackson square dance-type records. And Howdy Forrester had a couple of them out. So that's where I learned a lot of my tunes from. And as you travel around a little more, which I did, you just pick up stuff from other fiddlers. But they were all big influences, all those Texas fiddlers. Then of course bluegrass came along, and all of those fiddlers — Kenny Baker, Chubby Wise, all the Bill Monroe fiddlers.

You recorded three sides with Monroe, right before you went off to the Army — "Virginia Darling," "Gold Rush," and "Sally Goodin'." Do you remember anything in particular about that session?

I remember the whole thing, really. It was quite an exciting moment for me to be able to do that. I remember we all stood in a semi-circle, each of us had our own mic, and we had three hours to do it in. They were very strict in Nashville, you know, they went by the clock, and they tried to get a song an hour, which they did. We wanted to do "Train 45." We had that ready to record and we ran out of time. Now you can just book the studio as long as you want, but that's the way they did it back in those days. A three-hour slot and that's it — you do all you can in three hours... But we just stood in a semi-circle, and it was interesting the way it came out. We didn't use any earphones or anything like that, we just stood up there and played.

After you left Bill Monroe and went into the Army, did you continue to play?

I was lucky enough to get to play for a colonel who liked country music. In fact, it was about the fifth week of basic training that they had a thing called "Family Day," and they wanted to get together a little band from our company, so they put me in charge of that. There weren't any musicians in that whole company that you could say were musicians. So I asked my company commander if I could get some people to come help me play, and he says, "Hey, you're running it, you do what you want." So I called up the Stone Mountain Boys out of Dallas — Alan Munde was playing banjo with them at the time, and they were guys I had jammed with a lot when I was in college. So they brought a fiddle over for me, this one Saturday morning, and we played for our company, and there was this colonel, Colonel Reed, and he loved country music. He heard us play and he just flipped out about it, and came running over, saying, "Oh, gosh, you've got to play for the General, you got to do this, you got to do that." So he told the General, and I ended up playing for the Officer's Ball about the next week. I didn't get to use [the Stone Mountain Boys] — I just played by myself pretty much — I think there were some people from

> *"You should look forward to practicing. And if you use that word 'practice,'*
> *some kids don't like that word. 'I'm going to* play *now.' That sounds better."*

Special Services there. That's what I wanted to do, get into Special Services, and luckily it all worked out. They put me in Special Services, so I just stayed there, Fort Polk, Louisiana, for almost two years, which I was thankful to do, during that time. Doug Dillard called me the day before I got out of the Army, and asked me to come out and record. I had intended to go back to Nashville. But I went out [to California]. I was out there four days and ended up doing other session work, movie scores and what have you, and they wanted me to move out there, too, so that's what I did.

And after you got out here, the session work really took off for you.

Yeah, well the Rolling Stones thing helped.

That's probably the first time I heard you play, on [the Rolling Stones] album Let It Bleed *in '69 — "Country Honk."*

Gram Parsons suggested to them to get me to play on it, and I just barely knew him. This was in October of '69, about the same time. But anyway, I was back in Oklahoma here, getting ready to move out there on a permanent basis, and they called me up one evening and wanted me to come out. So they flew me out, picked me up, and we went up in the Hollywood Hills there — they had a house rented, and we stayed there for a few minutes, then we went down to the studio, Electra Studios, in L.A. I was in the studio for a couple of passes through, and they said, "Hey, we want you to come in, we want to talk to you," and I thought, oh, they don't like it, they're going to dump it. But I went in and they said, "We want you to stand outside in the street on the sidewalk and record it — we'll get a nice ambiance, we think," and I kind of giggled and said, "Well, whatever you want to do." So that's what we did. That's where they got the car horn.

What was it like to go from being in the presence of guys like Eck Robertson, Benny Thomasson, folks like that, and playing with the Dillards and Monroe, to playing with the rockers?

Well, it was a big change. The music is closely related, but you had to really study it in a way. Be able to improvise enough to get by with it. And naturally, playing with Monroe, I listened as much as I could to his past recordings, to see what those fiddlers did, how they approached it. You couldn't just get up there and start sawing away. You had to stay with the melody, and do what he wanted. He'd let you know if something was really off line. But for me he was easy to work with. Other people won't say that, but I had a good time with him. He just loved the old time tunes. He always featured me on the Grand Ol' Opry every time we got on there — he'd have a fiddle tune.

He always spoke highly of the Bluegrass Boys, too, and gave them room to play. What he would say, I heard, was that he liked to keep all the right things in bluegrass music.

Well, he had his way of playing it, and that was his prerogative — if he wanted it a certain way, then that's the way it was.

Do you have a regular practice routine that you go through, or do you pick it up and just play?

No, our band practices once a week, we try to every week, and work up new material and go over things. We just enjoy it, we make it a fun thing — I think that's the way practice ought to be. You should look forward to practicing. And if you use that word "practice," some kids don't like that word. " I'm going to *play* now." That sounds better.

Discography

Solo Albums:
- *Fiddle and a Song,* 1995, Sugar Hill 3838
- *Jumpin' the Strings,* 1991, Sugar Hill 3787
- *Double Trouble* (with John Hickman), 1986, Sugar Hill 3750
- *Outrageous,* 1981, Flying Fish
- *Dad's Favorites,* 1979, Rounder 0100
- *Pickin' and Fiddlin'* (with the Dillards), 1964, Elektra

Group Albums:
- Byron Berline Band, *Live at the Music Hall,* 1997, DSM 001

- California, *California Traveler,* 1992, Sugar Hill 3803
- BCH, *Now They Are Four,* 1991, Sugar Hill 3773
- BCH, *B.C.H.,* 1986, Sugar Hill 3755A
- BCH, *Night Run,* 1984, Sugar Hill 3739
- BCH, *Berline, Crary, Hickman,* 1981, Sugar Hill 3720
- L.A. Fiddle Band, *B. Berline & L.A. Fiddle Band,* 1980, Sugar Hill 3716
- Sundance, *Live at McCabe's,* 1979, Takoma 7061
- Sundance, *Byron Berline & Sundance,* 1977, MCA

- Country Gazette, *Live at McCabe's,* 1974
- Country Gazette, *Don't Give Up Your Day Job,* 1973, UA
- Country Gazette, *Traitor in Our Midst,* 1972, UA

For information on bookings, recordings, the Double Stop Music Shop, the International Bluegrass Festival, or Byron's custom videos, please contact him at 121 E. Oklahoma, Guthrie, OK 73044, (405) 282-6646. Website: http://www.doublestop.com

Sugar Hill Records, P.O. Box 55300, Durham, NC 27717; (800) 996-4455; http://www.sugarhillrecords.com

Jumpin' the Strings

By Byron Berline. Transcribed by Jack Tuttle as played by Byron Berline on his *Jumpin' the Strings* CD (Sugar Hill 3787).
(Also transcribed in Mel Bay's *Jumpin' the Strings* — transcriptions of all twenty-two of Byron's tunes from the album.)

A Chat With Kevin Burke

By Donna Maurer

Photo: Owen Carey

Recently I had the opportunity to talk with Kevin Burke. What a thrill! After all, he's one of the foremost Irish fiddlers living in the United States. Born of Irish immigrants, Kevin grew up in London's Irish community, and learned to play fiddle from some of the greatest Irish musicians living at that time.

Kevin has inspired lots of fiddlers — including myself — through his fiddle-playing in concerts, albums, instructional tapes and workshops. His early work with the Bothy Band still sounds fresh. In the past few years, Kevin has played in concert with the bands Patrick Street, Celtic Fiddle Festival (with Scottish fiddler Johnny Cunningham and Breton fiddler Christian LeMaitre), and his Open House band (with Mark Graham, Paul Kotapish and stepdancer Sandy Silva). Due to repeated requests from his audiences, Kevin is now planning a series of solo concert tours to take place over the next few years. Kevin took a moment to chat with me after the Folk Alliance Festival in Portland, Oregon, where he makes his home...

How did you get involved in playing Irish fiddle?

Well, both my parents came from the area known as Sligo, an area that has a strong tradition of fiddle playing. It was their idea to get me taught how to play, because they enjoyed the music. They never learned to play themselves, and they both kind of regretted it. So they didn't want me to grow up without having the chance to play music. So that set me for music lessons. I grew up in London, so they thought the best way to go about me learning the music was to have me sent to regular music classes, and then once I knew how to handle the instrument, I could then learn about how to play Irish music. So it wasn't my idea at all. They sent me off to music lessons early, at about seven or eight. And I didn't really get interested in it until I was about twelve or thirteen. And of course by that time, I could play a bit already. By the time I wanted to play, I was able to play. Kind of lucky!

What was the Irish music scene like when you were growing up in London?

I was really lucky that way. My parents had lots of friends who could play really well. In London in the early sixties, if you wanted to pick, say, your top five players of nearly any instrument in the Irish world, three or four of those top five guys were probably living in London. Like the fiddle players who were living there: Bobby Casey, Sean McGuire, Brendan McGlinchy, Michael Gorman, Martin Byrnes...that's just off the top of my head. There were loads more. So I had access to loads of Irish music all the time I was growing up. Probably as much as any kid in Ireland.

Some of those people that you named, would you say that they were the ones who influenced your style?

Yes. When I was a kid, I couldn't go out much, of course, and most of the sessions were in pubs. So I listened to a lot of records...The records I listened to were mainly Paddy Killoran, Michael Coleman and Hughie Gillespie. When I got a little bit older, I listened a lot to Brendan McGlinchy, Bobby Casey, Sean Maguire, Martin Byrnes, and I played a lot with a Sligo man called Tommy McGowan. He's a family friend, and he taught me a lot.

Would you say you are more of a Sligo player, or a Clare style player, or something else?

I really don't know the answer to that. I wouldn't say I'm a Sligo player, really. It was definitely the primary influence when I was a kid, but a lot of those guys I just mentioned played a different kind of music from the music played in Sligo. And I learned bits and pieces from all of them. So it would be wrong to say I'm a "purebred," you know? I've learned lots of different things from lots of different people.

Nowadays, how would you describe your style? Would you say it is pure Irish, or would you say it's a mix?

It's definitely Irish, I'd say. I never strayed too far from it. I often think that even when I'm playing other kinds of music, it still sounds kind of Irish. I don't really think in those terms. I'm more interested in the music side of it than I am...I have to make sure this doesn't sound wrong: If you take the phrase "Irish music", it's the "music" part that I'm interested in, more than the "Irish" part. I think it's a great form of music, and it comes from Ireland. My family comes from Ireland, and my culture is Irish. I have a lot of affection and respect for things Irish. But like I said, I grew up in London and I can't pretend I didn't. And I heard all these different players and

*"It's always a puzzle...There's always this effort to find more or do it
again, or 'how would it work this way?' A never-ending curse!"*

different styles of music, and that's definitely the heaviest influence that I have... I'm just a bit cautious about saying "Yes, I'm Irish," because the fact is I'm not, but I'm pretty close to it. I definitely consider myself a lot more Irish than I would English. How that transfers musically, I'm not sure.

In the time that you've been playing, what changes have you seen in Irish music?

Well, when I came to this country first, most people didn't seem to know what Irish music meant. Here, the phrase "Irish music" meant nothing. I don't think that's the case anymore, because of groups like the Chieftains, the Bothy Band, and Planxty. Just the increased communication all around. People have a much better idea of what Irish music sounds like. In Ireland, I think the main difference is that people can grow up and become musicians for a living. When I was I kid, like all those guys that I'd mentioned, hardly any of them were full-time musicians. Most of them had other jobs, trying to raise a family. But the traditional music has developed so much that it is possible to make a living playing music now...Another difference is that it has left the kitchen and entered the concert hall....

What type of playing situations — sessions, solo, with a group, recording, live performance, or teaching — which of those types of situations do you enjoy most, and why?

Well, the best of all situations is a couple of friends in a quiet place, like a bar or a house, where you can just play and enjoy yourself without having to bother anyone else! But having said that, it's nice to play in a concert hall and see all these people ready, willing and able to enjoy this music that twenty-five years ago would have been foreign to them. The recording studio is for me really intense. It wears me down, and I find it difficult. I find it really hard work. I do it mainly as a challenge. It's not something I enjoy. I mean I do enjoy it in a way, I don't see it as forced. I see it as something that's difficult and takes a lot of hard work, and is very challenging. I view it all in those terms. I definitely go to bed at night tired. After a week or two in the studio, I'm usually pretty burned out. Teaching, I find that tiring, too, but not as much as recording. I kind of enjoy trying to help other people to learn how to play this kind of stuff.

Besides Open House, you've played with the Celtic Fiddle Festival, Patrick Street, the Bothy Band, and other people. What effect did these and other different situations have on your playing?

I try to look at every piece of music as a piece of music, divorced from everything. I try to make it work in itself. If it sounds okay to me, then I regard it as a success. Nearly everything I play that is not Irish, I like to let it be obvious that I have a lot of respect for what I'm trying to play. But on the other hand, I'd like to have a bit of respect back. I'm not trying to convince anybody that I'm from Scandinavia. When I play a Scandinavian tune, I know full well that I'm not going to sound like a Norwegian fiddle player. But I don't think that should bar me from trying to play that kind of music, since the only reason I'm playing it is because I find it attractive. I hope I do it justice, but obviously for the purist it might be slightly irritating. I'd rather make a good effort than ignore the thing altogether. I listen to a lot of different kinds of music. I don't want to feel like I'm not allowed to play [any of it].

You've been playing for quite some time. How do you keep your interest going in playing Irish music?

I don't know. It's not really an effort. It's always a puzzle. I think if you talk to any musician, they'll tell you the same. There's always this effort to find more or do it again, or "how would it work this way?" A never-ending curse!

Discography

Feature Titles:
• *Kevin Burke in Concert* (Green Linnet — solo album planned for 1999)
• *If the Cap Fits* (GL 3009)
• *Up Close* (GL 1052)
• *Eavesdropper* (with Jackie Daly) (GL 3002)
• *Promenade* (GL 3010)
• *Portland* (with Mícheál Ó Domhnaill) (GL 1041)

Celtic Fiddle Festival:
• *Encore* (GL 1189)
• *Celtic Fiddle Festival* (GL 1133)

Patrick Street:
• *Live From Patrick Street* (GL 1194)
• *Corner Boys* (GL 1160)
• *Made in Cork* (GL 1184)
• *Patrick Street* (GL 1071)
• *No. 2 Patrick Street* (GL 1088)
• *Irish Times* (GL1105)
• *All In Good Time* (GL1125)

Open House:
• *Open House* (GL1122)
• *Second Story* (GL 1144)
• *Hoof & Mouth* (GL 1169)

Instructional Videos:
Learn to Play Irish Fiddle I & II (Homespun)

Green Linnet Records, Inc., (203) 730-0333

Homespun Tapes, (800) 33-TAPES/(914) 246-2550

Bookings for Kevin Burke: Maureen Brennan, (510) 556-9803.

U.S. bookings for Patrick Street: Herschel Freeman, (901) 757-4567

European bookings for Patrick Street: Ad Astra, 44-1377-217622

The Long Acre

By Kevin Burke. From his *Open House* CD (Green Linnet GL 1122).

Clyde's Banks

By Kevin Burke. From his *Open House* CD (Green Linnet GL 1122).

Vassar Clements: Bridging the Gap from Bill Monroe to Jerry Garcia

By Jack Tuttle

Since first appearing with Bill Monroe and the Blue Grass Boys in 1949, Vassar Clements has become one of the true giants of the bluegrass world. Although his early recordings reflect a fairly mainstream bluegrass sound, by the '60s and '70s, Vassar had developed a wild jazzy sound that made him the first great progressive fiddler to emerge from the bluegrass field.

After appearing on two landmark albums of the 1970s, the Nitty Gritty Dirt Band's Will The Circle Be Unbroken *and* Old And In The Way *with Jerry Garcia and David Grisman, Vassar attracted legions of bluegrass/hippie/jazz types who were turned on to the aggressive, somewhat crazed sounds that had never before been heard from a fiddle. Featuring continuously shifting double stops on all parts of the neck, chromatic runs and jarring offbeat phrasings, Vassar came to be the most easily recognized bluegrass fiddle player in the business.*

Since those days, Vassar has kept one foot planted firmly in the bluegrass world, the other in the jazz world. Now usually found fronting his own band, Vassar is still often called upon for special appearances both live and on recordings from such diverse performers as Linda Ronstadt, Tony Rice, and the Rolling Stones. This interview took place at the Warfield in San Francisco in March, 1996.

Why don't we talk a little about your beginning career on the fiddle, and what possessed you to take up the instrument?

It's hard to say what possessed me... I didn't have any training, I didn't have anybody to show me. My step-father got a guitar and a fiddle, maybe the guitar was a little bit before, but it was right close to the same time. He got a guitar and a fiddle from a used furniture store and brought them to the house. Nobody knew anything about it. I didn't know what you were supposed to do with it, or that you were supposed to put rosin on the bow or anything else. And so I tried to learn guitar and fiddle about the same time [when I was seven years old]. And something just kept drawing me to the fiddle. Every time I'd see the two instruments, I'd go to the fiddle.

Did you put a lot of time in?

A lot of time.

Hours and hours every day?

Yeah, because the first thing, I just had to figure out what to do. It took forever to do that. I'd get to listen to the radio maybe an hour on Saturday night and hear the Grand Ole Opry, and I heard what one was supposed to sound like, but I didn't know how to make it sound like that.

How long did it take before you started getting some good music out of it?

Oh, I wouldn't let anybody know I was even trying, except my mother, around the house there. At first I found out you had to put rosin on the bow to make any sound on the strings. And then I had to get tunes that I would hear on the Opry in my head, and just pick them out a note for a note. Da, da, da, you know, stuff like that.

But you had no way to tape them or anything...

No, no. Not back then. We had a battery radio. I'd never heard of a tape recorder.

"I grew up with big bands...and it sounded like their music was just flowing, like water, and I was trying to make the fiddle do that."

A lot of fiddle tunes go by pretty quickly, to store them in your mind...

Oh, they go by fast! But if somebody would sing something, you know, when you're a kid you can remember things better, and I'd have these tunes in my mind — not fiddle tunes...

So they were more singing pieces that you were playing.

Yeah, because these fiddle tunes would go by so fast, I didn't know what was happening. But Roy Acuff or somebody like Red Foley would sing a song, and I'd kind of keep the melody.

When did you sort of venture out and start playing in front of people?

Oh, let's see, I was probably ten or eleven years old. Somebody at school found out that I was trying to play, or learning to play. And they thought it was great. I thought they'd look down on me, you know, "What in the world is he doing playing that old stuff?" And then I got to trying to play for square dances and stuff like that.

You tend to use longer bow strokes than a lot of people...

Yeah, and I guess it's because I taught myself, I don't know. I was trying to make it flow. I grew up with big bands, listening to that stuff, and it sounded like their music was just flowing, like water, and I was trying to make the fiddle do that.

When did you start getting out — was Bill Monroe your first big job?

Yeah, he was the first one. I can't remember how old I was — I was still in high school. And I'd get homesick and go back home. That was my first time away from home. But I met him when he came through Florida. My step-father knew Chubby Wise, who was playing fiddle with him. And once or twice he got him to come over to the house. And I wouldn't even try to play fiddle or anything, because Chubby — ooh, play fiddle around him? But I could play rhythm guitar a little bit, and I just sat in there with them. So that's the way that all started. I came to find out that Monroe was looking for a fiddle player, and my mother let me go up there. I had a round-trip ticket, and probably fifty cents in my pocket. And I got the job.

Were you pretty comfortable with that? Were you sure you could do it?

No, I wasn't comfortable with it. No, I was scared to death. I knew his tunes, his songs, but I didn't know any breakdowns. I knew "Orange Blossom Special" and "Old Joe Clark" and "Boil Them Cabbage Down" and "Rubber Dolly." And when I auditioned for him, he would call off these songs for me to play them. And I knew all the songs, because I had copied Chubby. And he says, "Do you know any breakdowns?" And I said, "A few." And he said, "Do you know 'Orange Blossom Special'?" He happened to hit the one I knew. So he didn't ask for any after that. I just kind of bluffed my way through, and he took me under his wing and showed me a lot of stuff.

You have a very distinctive, very progressive style of playing. At this point, had you developed that yet, or were you pretty straight with your playing?

No, I hadn't developed it. I still haven't. It's a never-ending thing. But I think subconsciously, big band things I had heard would come out of my instrument, even though it was bluegrass or whatever.

It seems like on the recordings you did with Monroe back then, you sound pretty much like his other fiddle players did at that point.

Yeah, when I started, I copied Chubby, every note. But then when he did new tunes, I didn't have Chubby to go by, so I had to do it my way. So I don't really remember how they turned out. But I started getting, I guess, my own style of things. I know now that it was, but then I didn't know it. I didn't know if it sounded like somebody else or what.

Had you started writing at that point?

No, I think the first tune I ever wrote was that "Lonesome Fiddle Blues."

Pretty good first tune!

Yeah, I don't know how it ever came about. It just happened. I played that thing all the time.

When you were learning, did you ever do any exercises or anything to make your fingers work better, or your bow arm, or did you just play tunes, songs?

Well, I don't think I did exercises as much as I tried to do little riffs and make them fit. And you'd get to the point where you'd think you weren't learning anything, so you'd just reverse where you were hitting and see if that would work, just anything, to see if you could get a different sound.

Did you struggle with your left hand at all when you were playing some of the complicated passages, or did it just come sort of naturally?

Nothing comes easy. It seems like it was a never-ending struggle, and still is. There's so much on there, you know. The bow has to be working with the left hand and you can't think about it. It just all has to go together.

Do you sometimes hear your own licks coming out of [the younger fiddle players around today]?

Yeah. At the beginning, I said, "Where did that come from? I've heard that." But I knew I must have gotten it from a big band or something. It's a compliment for me for somebody to do something like that.

Do you have advice you can give to students?

Yeah, don't ever give up. Don't ever give up. Because it will make you want to. A fiddle will just make you so mad, you'll cry and everything else. But just don't quit.

Selected Discography

- *Will the Circle Be Unbroken* (United Artists)
- *Vassar* (Mercury)
- *Superbow* (Mercury)
- *Southern Waltzes* (Rhythm Records)
- *Vassar Clements, John Hartford & Dave Holland* (Rounder)
- *Crossing the Catskills* (Rounder)
- *Vassar Clements* (MCA)
- *Bluegrass Sessions* (Flying Fish)
- *Vassar* (Flying Fish)
- *Grass Routes* (Rounder)
- *Saturday Night Shuffle – A Celebration of Merle Travis* (Shanachie)
- *Hillbilly Jazz* (Flying Fish)
- *Hillbilly Jazz Rides Again* (Flying Fish)
- *New Hillbilly Jazz* (Shikata)

- *Together At Last* (with Stéphane Grappelli) (Flying Fish)
- *Nashville Jam* (Flying Fish)
- *Westport Drive* (Mind Dust Records)
- *The Man, The Legend* (Vassillie Productions)
- *Country Classics* (Vassillie Productions)
- *Vassar Clements Reunion with the Dixie Gentlemen* (Old Homestead)
- *Once In A While* (jam with Miles Davis' ex-band members) (Flying Fish)
- *Live in Telluride 1979* (Vassillie Productions)
- *Music City USA* (Vassillie Productions)
- *Old And In The Way, vol. 1* (BMG Music)
- *Old And In The Way – That High Lonesome Sound, vol. 2* (Acoustic Disc)
- *An Americana Christmas* (with Norman Blake) (Winter Harvest)

- *Vassar's Jazz (Golden Anniversary)* (Winter Harvest)

Videos:
- *Vassar Clements Fiddle Instruction Tapes* (Homespun Tapes)
- *Vassar Clements in Concert (Vassar Swings)* (Shikata Records)
- *Vassar Clements in Concert (Ramblin' 810)* (Shanachie Records)

Many of the above recordings and videos are available from Vassillie Productions, P.O. Box 567, Hermitage, TN 37076; (888) 222-9505; website: http://www.mbus.com/vassar or http://www.vassarclements.com
Email: VASSARSMUSIC@worldnet.att.net

Take A Break

By Vassar and Millie Clements, © Vassar's Music, ASCAP. Transcribed by Jack Tuttle as
played by Vassar on his *Vassar's Jazz, Golden Anniversary Album* CD (Winter Harvest WH 3311-2)

Michael Doucet: Hot Cajun Fiddle!

By Niles Hokkanen

Michael Doucet has a metaphysical mission in life: to absorb, understand and "grok" the entire spectrum of Cajun and related music, past and present, and its relation to the culture which spawned it, and then, with that firm foundation, to add his own contributions to it. While getting his fiddle chops together, Doucet sought out the most important Cajun fiddlers of the previous generations to learn from directly. Forming BeauSoleil in 1976, Michael has been the driving force which has made it the premier Cajun band of recent history. Through various personnel changes and record labels (Swallow, Arhoolie, Rounder, Rhino), BeauSoleil has sought to present a total Cajun music experience, performing unaccompanied ballads, old obscure fiddle tunes, accordion-driven rave-ups, zydeco smokers, and so on.

You started playing fiddle relatively "late," at least the classical people would say so.

I was basically in my early twenties. My uncle had a fiddle, and in high school I could play three songs on it. But that was "rub-a-dub-dub." It wasn't until I was about twenty-one that I decided I was going to play fiddle. I went to France and came back and then kind of played/practiced eight hours a day or whatever it took…got really serious about it. But it just came naturally.

You went out and studied with a lot of the older players, maybe that was a function of your adult mind. Let's go down the list and maybe you could say what particular thing(s) you learned from each… The Balfa Brothers?

Will Bolfa was the "seconding" and the rhythm. He had the best accompaniment — it was just so smooth. Will would hardly ever use his little finger, just the first three. He emphasized the rhythm with his fingering of his left hand rather than with the bow. He'd slide into the notes. Hector Duhon [Dixie Ramblers] was the rhythmic thing, too. Hector was the first, study-wise. He would really show how to "second." Now Will would second a lot lower — under the first fiddle; Hector seconded (played backup) as the sole fiddle in his band. He could really squeeze into the notes and use accents and slides. He used a lot of slides in the middle chordal positions. Dewey Balfa had so much…The bowing, a really smooth bowing. He had a real nice tone. I think Dewey was just the smoothest and perhaps the easiest to learn from because he could verbalize as well as analyze what he was doing.

Varise Connor …

Oh, talk about *smooth!* My God, "Mr. Glass." Varise was definitely the bow arm. He had the most amazing bow arm. He really showed me about which direction to play a note. There's a way to play across strings, kind of a shuffle that goes over a three-string chord. Stuff like that. How to really bow, and intonation. Varise had *the* intonation. Lionel Leleux would play in standard tuning and accompany a C accordion. He had that down and he had a real good bow, a great violin, and a deep tone.

Canray Fontenot and Bébé Carrière? And keep going …

Bébé was the blues. Canray — definitely the rhythms and just wildness and making the fiddle speak and getting sounds out of it to represent your emotions…how to make a violin cry. Rufus Thibodeaux carries the finesse of country and swing. Rufus played a lot like Harry Choates. From him, the country/swing aspect of being improvisational and the clarity of the notes and getting the most sound out. Doc Guidry was chordal. Doc really played the chords well, but he also kept the rhythm with the bow. Like I was trying to explain how Hector and Will Bolfa kept the rhythm with their left hand fingers, Doc kept the rhythm more with the bow.

And, of course, Dennis McGee.

From Dennis, it was *everything*. With Dennis, it was to relearn how to play Cajun music because those songs were so old, predating electricity and cars and gasoline engines. It went back to a different rhythmic time. With Dennis, you had to relearn everything because he played it so differently. His rhythms were so different; it could be the same song I'd learned from somebody else, but it might be in a different key or a different way of bowing it. It would go against the grain if you didn't play it (with him) the way he played or with the same rhythm. And from Dennis, it's also the repertoire. He had heard the first people doing these songs — he was not one to learn those things off of records! [Laughs.]

*"I'm not trying to be Dewey Balfa or Dennis McGee or whoever, but all those
are there because I've experienced so much, and the experience was French...."*

Cajun music has various styles within it. Could you talk about the major sub-styles, and if those are from different geographical areas, etc.?

This is going to be tough. First, what you have now is not what you would have found ten years ago, which is what you wouldn't have found ten years before that, and ten years before that. You find remnants of earlier styles. Let's do this thing historically. If you have the *Beau Solo* CD, there's a song on that called "Valse Acadienne" — that is what Acadian music sounded like; that's the earliest stuff — very droney, no accordion. It's in A-E-A-E tuning. Dennis [McGee] would come under that style. That died out with Dennis as far as I'm concerned; true players, though — maybe Wade Frugé — might play something like that.

Then let's go to a Luderin Darbonne [Hackberry Ramblers] or string band style. That was in the '30s. That was from west Louisiana and anytime you're closer to Texas, you pick up a lot of that influence. Some of those Texas waltzes are Cajunized, as are some of those two-steps or polkas from those Bohemian or Czech or whatever bands they had out there. Now, to follow through with that even more would be Harry Choates…much more western swing. So western Louisiana tended to be more swingy, country influenced.

Then Eunice, which is the head or capital of the prairie. Eunice let's say would be more accordion-influenced and that would change the fiddle styles. Also, at the same time, that's where you had Amédé Ardoin and a lot of black players who play *Cajun* music, who don't play what we call zydeco and don't play rhythm & blues, but rather play old-style music. People like Bébé Carrière, Calvin Carrière; they play along with the diatonic accordion but that style is another kind of thing…more bluesy.

Then you have a Lafayette style which is a mixture. You have Doc Guidry who played early with Happy Fats, played country style, but still Cajun, a lot of rhythmic things. Another player who rose up from him is Rufus (Thibodeaux); he is the best known.

Now Doug Kershaw, he's from that area of Mermentau, close to Texas. I really love Doug's early stuff — it's so funky and earthy. Just wild and raw.

What about the Balfa Brothers?

The Balfas learned a lot from accordionist Nathan Abshire who came from Kaplan. They said they learned a lot from their father. That really neat waltz, "Valse à Balfa" is actually a ballad that Dewey learned from his aunt or one of the sisters. A lot of their style came from ballads. Now the straight-ahead fiddle sound — that's unique, but that's a fiddle sound of twin playing, which kind of goes back to… they heard a lot of Harry Choates, The Hackberry Ramblers, and probably The Dixie Ramblers. So everyone after that, including the Balfas, was definitely influenced by records, by 78s. The early Balfa style, what you hear on that record *The Balfa Brothers Play Traditional Cajun Music,* which is my favorite, is a lot of accordion songs played on fiddle.

So it's not the regions — it's the people. You have to go by "the heads of state," or people who may have had bands. It might not have been just the styles from them, but they are good proponents. The people created the style; the style is from the region. But the region may have a lot to do with what those individuals around whom the music evolves were exposed to.

So how varied or traditional are the influences which go into your own playing?

I don't incorporate anything that wasn't here before. Everything I play is learned from Louisiana. I went back in time — not only to French music, but to blues, jazz, popular music, Irish music, whatever was there. As more old recordings are brought to light, you can see these influences and what a hotbed Louisiana was.

If you listen to early New Orleans music, clarinet and violin played about the same thing, so you can listen to early New Orleans clarinet players and get fiddle lines. This is before Sidney Bechet. A.J. Piron was a great New Orleans violin player and he played along with Lorenzo Tio, who was a great clarinetist. I met an early '20s style jazz fiddle player, Bradford Gordon from Opelousas, and he said, "Oh yeah, I showed this guy Leo Soileau how to play fiddle. Ever heard of him?" He played all this swingy, jazz stuff. So, my influences are the spectrum of Louisiana music.

There are some songs that you just want to play as close as you can [to the way you learned them], and that's the way it is supposed to be. There's no variance, no improvisation, because the song is so powerful in itself. Then, there are the skeletons of songs that lend themselves to reworking, that you can do in different styles. What I find satisfying is to try to write new songs. On the last two albums, I've done some writing in the style, but it's not copping licks. It's writing new songs but doing so in the language that you learned how to play the stuff in the first place, where maybe only the old people can really understand what you're doing and saying. I know, through these songs, I'm talking to these guys who died; I'm talking to this society, through 300 years of hardship, from being an Acadian. Writing a new song within the style — that takes some time.

You can look at the music; the music is simple. But what about the feeling, and why do you play this thing in a certain way? Is it a certain person that you have heard, or am I being something different? Is something else coming through? This way, since I'm not copying anybody... I'm not trying to be Dewey Balfa or Dennis McGee or whoever, but all those are there because I've experienced so much, and the experience was French. The experience was being put down, being told, "Oh man, you don't want to play that stuff." Remember what the music was like in the '60s and early '70s when it was just played in bars and sometimes out of tune and in a party atmosphere...the whole stereotype. But, at the same time, it was great. And to go out and find that beauty and to find people like Varise Connor, who hadn't played in thirty years, who asked, "Why are you interested in me?" And I said, "Because you're an incredible fiddle player!" [Laughs.]

It's the experience, it's not just the notes. It's hard to get that when you just listen to commercial records, whether they are field recordings or not, although they are good. But you are just "hearing" it; you're not understanding what kind of environment this thing came from, 'cause it's *so different.*

You like to present variety on your recordings.

There's so much stuff in Louisiana. We could do so many different records of music, so many different styles. Most of the records that we've done, you can find a ballad, a fiddle tune (probably from Dennis), some old songs, whatever. But that's our [BeauSoleil's] own tradition; we're the only ones that do that. If I'm going to make a record, there are the categories that it should have, which is what I've been doing for over twenty years. You could take some pretty cool songs, other (non-Cajun) songs, and Cajunize them (we did that before), but why? I don't have to do that now. You mature, you're within this culture and understand it and the new stuff shouldn't be from somewhere else; it should be from you....

Discography

With Beausoleil:
- *Allons à Lafayette* (Arhoolie 308)
- *Arc de Triomph Two-Step* (1st recording, from France, 1976) (EMI-72438592722)
- *Bayou Boogie* (Rounder 6015)
- *Bayou Cadillac* (Rounder 6025)
- *Bayou Deluxe: The Best of Michael Doucet & Beausoleil* (Rhino 71169)
- *Best of Beausoleil* (Arhoolie 458)
- *Belizaire the Cajun* (soundtrack) (Arhoolie 5038)
- *Cajun Brew* (Rounder 6017)
- *Cajun Conja* (Rhino 70525)
- *Christmas Bayou* (Swallow Records 6064)
- *Danse de la Vie* (Rhino 71221)
- *Déjà Vu* (Swallow Records 6080)
- *Dit Beausoleil* (Arhoolie 5025)
- *Hot Chili Mama* (Arhoolie 5040)
- *L'echo* (Rhino 71808)
- *L'amour ou la Folie* (1998 Grammy winner) (Rhino 72622)
- *Le Hoogie Boogie/Louisiana French Music for Children* (Rounder 8022)
- *Live! From the Left Coast* (Rounder 6035)
- *Louisiana Cajun Music* (formerly titled *Beausoleil, the Spirit of Cajun Music*) (Swallow Records 6031)
- *The Mad Reel* (Arhoolie 397)
- *Parlez-Nous A Boire* (Arhoolie 322)
- *Vintage Beausoleil* (Music of the World 213)
- *Zydeco Gris-Gris* (Swallow Records 6054)

With Various Other Artists:
- *Beau Solo* (with David Doucet) (Arhoolie 321)
- *Cajun Experience* (with P. Daigle, R. Elkins) (Swallow Records 6058)
- *Cajun Fiddle Styles, vol. 1* (with Canray Fontenot, Carrière Brothers) (Arhoolie 5031)
- *Cajun Gold, vol. 1* (with P. Daigle, R. Elkins) (Gold Band Records 7759)
- *Cajun Jam Session* (with A. Senauke, D. Poullard) (Arhoolie 5035)
- *Creole Crossroads* (with N. Williams) (Rounder 2137)
- *Ensemble Encore* (with O. Clark, H. Duhon) (Rounder 6011)
- *Grand Texas* (with Chuck Guillory) (Arhoolie 5039)
- *Highly Seasoned Cajun Music* (Coteau) (Rounder 6078)
- *Home Music* (Savoy-Doucet Cajun Band) (Arhoolie 5029)
- *Home Music With Spirits* (Savoy-Doucet Cajun Band) (Arhoolie 389)
- *Live! At the Dance* (Savoy-Doucet Cajun Band) (Arhoolie 418)
- *Louisiana Hot Sauce – Creole Style!* (Canray Fontenot, members of Beausoleil, others) (Arhoolie 381)
- *Masters of the Folk Violin –'94 tour* (Arhoolie 434)
- *"Oh, What a Night!"* (with Mark Savoy, others) (Arhoolie 5023)
- *Quand J'ai Parti* (David Doucet) (Rounder 6040)
- *Savoy-Doucet With Spirits* (Savoy-Doucet Cajun Band) (Arhoolie 5037)
- *Songs of Innocence & Experience* (with G. Brown) (Red House Records RHR-14)
- *Two Step d'Amédé* (Savoy-Doucet Cajun Band) (Arhoolie 316)
- *Un 'Tit Peu Plus Cajun* (Jimmy Breaux) (LL-1003)

Instructional Audio Tapes:
- *Learn to Play Real Cajun Fiddle* (Homespun)

Videos:
- *Learn to Play Cajun Fiddle* (Homespun)
- *Haunted Waters* (documentary, music by Michael Doucet) (9730, avail. through Glen Pitre's Louisiana Catalogue, (800) 375-4100.)

Rhino Records, (310) 474-4778, ext. 6281/80
Music of the World, Ltd., Box 3620, Chapel Hill, NC 27515
Red House Records, (612) 379-1089
Gold Band Records, (318) 439-8839
Rounder Records, (800) 443-4727
Arhoolie, (510) 525-7471
Homespun, (800) 33-TAPES/(914) 246-2550

Bookings: Rosebud Agency, (415) 386-3456
Mailing list/Fan club: Miss Beverly, 640 W. 231st St., Suite 1H, Riverdale, NY 10463. Note: please mark correspondence "Beausoleil."

Madame Etienne

Transcribed by Jack Tuttle.

"This waltz was first recorded in 1929 by Créole accordionist Amédé Ardoin and Cajun fiddler Dennis McGee. During the times we spent together, Dennis and I would often play this tune. The second fiddle part [on the recording] represents the older Acadian style of seconding." — Michael Doucet

Jackie Dunn:
Cape Breton Roots

By Mary Larsen

Jackie Dunn grew up in Antigonish County, Nova Scotia, not far from Cape Breton. Jackie has strong ties to the music and people of Cape Breton, including such fiddling relatives as the late John Willie MacEachern (her grandfather), the late Alex Joe MacEachern and Dan Hughie MacEachern (her grand uncles). Her extended family also includes Howie MacDonald, Theresa, Marie and Donald MacLellan, David MacIsaac, and Angus and Maybelle Chisholm.

Jackie began step dancing at age four, learning from and performing with her mother, Margaret MacEachern Dunn. At age five, Jackie began studying classical piano. At eight, she took up the fiddle, studying with Stan Chapman. She was soon performing solo on the fiddle, as well as step dancing and accompanying other fiddlers on the piano. In her teens, Jackie performed extensively throughout Cape Breton and the Maritime provinces, as well as in Vancouver at Expo '86, and Ontario and the northeast U.S. She has appeared on television and radio numerous times. In March 1998, Jackie played at the San Francisco Celtic Festival with Wendy MacIsaac and Gordie Samson; this was followed by performances in Philadelphia and Delaware. The summer of 1998 found her at the Gaelic College on the Isle of Skye, Scotland, teaching fiddle along with Buddy MacMaster. Back home in Cape Breton, Jackie is an elementary school music teacher. She also teaches fiddle privately and in groups.

Do you do any fiddle or piano in your classes?

I'm starting a fiddle program. I got it going last year, and all my fiddles are in this year, so I'm pretty serious about it. It starts in grade three, but it's really basic at that age. Grades four to seven do a little bit better with it. They're working on some jigs and some reels.

Do you have any teaching tips for children learning?

I think just to listen to as much fiddling as they can — different age fiddlers, and styles, so they don't just go by… I think the tendency now is for the little kids to look to the people who are commercially successful, and they think that's the style. And it is the style, but it's a newer form. I'm just so traditional that I think they should be exposed to older people who may not even be living anymore. Like Donald Angus Beaton, and Dan R. MacDonald, and Dan Hughie MacEachern. I guess you could even go back further than that — they're sort of all in the same generation. But at least Buddy MacMaster's age, and before him. I think that we don't talk about the culture enough, the traditions, and the kids don't even know what they're missing if we don't point it out. They need to know where it came from and that what they're hearing now is just a new branch of it. And the same goes for adults — maybe they're coming into this new. They should look at different styles and create their own thing. That's so important in our style of fiddling — that individuals create their own style. They shouldn't try to copy someone's style, even if they really like that person — it's kind of a "no no."

How did you get started playing for dances and concerts?

When I was first in concerts, I was dancing, because my mother (Margaret MacEachern Dunn) was involved in putting concerts on. She would dance in a concert, and when I was really small I would come on at the end of her number and dance with her. When I became good enough to dance on my own, I got my own number in the Glendale concert, and different concerts around Cape Breton. I think maybe I was asked quite a bit because there weren't very many young people [playing or dancing] at the time. I'm sort of the older one of the group now, but I was one of the first ones then to play the fiddle. And I got started playing for sets, I think, because I played with Natalie [MacMaster] so much, and she was one of the first ones that started playing for dances. Later, we were all playing for dances — Rodney MacDonald, Wendy MacIsaac, Ashley MacIsaac and everyone, and we'd be mixed up — we'd play with different people every time.

Do you still play for a lot of dances?

Yes. Mostly everything I do is dances, and then the odd concert — at home, because I don't travel too much because of my job. So the weekends it's usually the dances we play for, at pubs — that's the main thing around Cape Breton.

"I think that we don't talk about the culture enough, the traditions, and the kids don't even know what they're missing if we don't point it out. They need to know where it came from and that what they're hearing now is just a new branch of it."

You believe that a knowledge of the Gaelic language can help fiddlers get the right rhythm and emphasis in their music — is it possible to find words to many of the old tunes, in Gaelic? Did you come across any in doing your thesis (on the relationship between the Gaelic language and Scottish and Cape Breton music)?

The ones that I heard or found, people had told the words to me, or recited them. I don't know if that's something that people are doing, writing them down. They should be written down before they're forgotten. But the ones that I know are the common ones that people sing, like you know the title is Gaelic, and you might know the first few words. The ones I'm thinking of are the strathspeys and reels, the mouth music pieces. Those are ones that probably, if you lived in Cape Breton, you would have heard them sometime in your life.

Were they actual words, or nonsensical syllables?

It could be one or the other, or a combination. Some of them did have actual words that had a story, and some of them didn't. And I think that's important. And maybe that's why I was saying people should listen to the older players, because those older players were Gaelic speakers, and there's just something different in their music — you can't really describe it, unless you could pick a tune and be shown, "here's the words, this is how they sound when you say them," and then look at the fiddler's playing of that same tune. But it's so abstract. I think just listening to their style, you might pick up those little things without having to talk about it.

Discography

Albums:
- *Dunn to a "T"* (1995)
- *In Jig Time* (Brenda Stubbert, 1995 — Jackie is piano accompanist)
- *Let 'er Rip* (Glenn Graham, 1996 — Jackie is piano accompanist)

Videos:
- *Carrying on the Traditions: Cape Breton Scottish Fiddling Today* (Fiddler Magazine Video FMV-03)
- *Cape Breton Island*
- *Cape Breton Island, Volume Two*
- *The Heart of the Gael*

- *The Highland Heart of Nova Scotia*

For bookings or to order *Dunn to a "T"*, contact Jackie at P.O. Box 138, Judique, N.S., Canada B0E 1P0, (902) 787-2117.

Jackie I Hardly Knew Ya

Composed by Jackie Dunn, from her album *Dunn to a "T"*

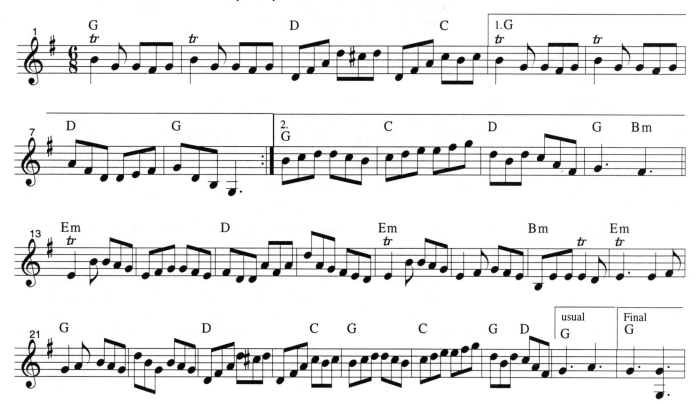

J.P. Fraley: The Fiddlers' Fiddler

By Bob Buckingham

For anyone who might not know, J.P. Fraley is probably the best-known fiddler from an area with a rich fiddle tradition — northeastern Kentucky. J.P. Fraley is a quiet man. He does not draw attention to himself. He is easy to miss in the crowd, except that he is usually in the center of a jam. It seems everyone wants to jam with J.P. and he usually wants to jam with them. Often, when he is jamming, he will play softly so he can hear the others around him.

He lost his wife Annadeene — his partner in life and music — a couple of years ago. While that space can never be filled, J.P. continues to be a remarkable presence. His daughter, Danielle, plays guitar so much like her mother that it is uncanny. She will accompany her father on a forthcoming CD from Rounder Records.

If you are fortunate enough to spend time with J.P., you may hear him singing or diddling tunes as he goes about his business. Rarely does time go by that he is not hearing music in his head. Additionally, he is a great storyteller and his stories are held in high regard; they ring with age-old truths laden with irony. Heck, they are downright funny.

I caught up with J.P. at his home in Denton, Kentucky — a log cabin in a 150-plus acre tract of land just a bit off the beaten path. It was a wonderfully warm November afternoon and he had invited some friends in for a cabin jam.

J.P., How long have you been playing the fiddle?

Since I was nine years old.

Where were you learning then?

Mostly on the front porch at home — my daddy was a fiddler —and occasionally from the local fiddlers. We didn't have a whole lot at the time. They would all gather on the porch and the only guitar player at the time was...we called him Monkey Bill Stevens. I used to beat straws for all the fiddlers when I first started, at about nine. Most of the tunes were played open or cross-keyed and you could beat on the D and G strings and get pretty good volume out of it. I know Daddy would have me do it. I know I'd get so tired I'd start hitting his fingers!

What part did fiddling play in the community? Even today you hear stories about Ed Haley and others.

Yeah, Ed Haley, even until today he was ahead of his time to me, and I was young and Daddy would take me to these stores, the wholesale house in Ashland or Catlettsburg. We'd find Ed playing on the street, you know, and Dad would put some money in his cup. I'd stand there, you know, until Ed stopped playing the fiddle. It kind of bugged me a little because people did not realize what they were listening to. They'd try to step on his feet and so forth. Now John Hartford is working to get some good quality recordings out of Ed Haley.[1] Those old home recordings were kind of comical. You see they had a cardboard core. And they'd get worn down to where you could hear the tune a little bit but then there'd be this curl of cardboard following the needle. That was the kind of records Rounder had to work with when they put out that LP.

When you were growing up, what role did fiddling play? Was it something people wanted to hear, or was it for dances, or what purpose did it have?

What really helped me back then, I did not realize it at the time, but during the Depression, Daddy ran a park. At the time Grayson [Kentucky] did not have a railhead. They did at one time, but during the Depression they did not. They had to depend on rail shipments coming into Hitchins. The circus and the carnivals, they traveled by rail. Especially the circus wagons and stuff. They would have the circus there at Hitchins where I grew up in my Daddy's park. And with these circuses and carnivals, it was surprising, good musicians

---

[1] *Ed Haley — Forked Deer* (Rounder 1131/1132) and *Grey Eagle* (Rounder 1133/1134)

"[Fiddling] got me out of a lot of work... [Daddy] had us hoeing corn. God, it was hot. I'd say, "Daddy, if I go on home, I believe I could play 'Sally Goodin.'" He said, "When you get to the end of the row there, set your hoe there and go on down and play the fiddle." My brothers were getting mad at me. They'd see me leave. I'd go down there, I'd get the fiddle out and play it about five minutes. Then I'd put it back under the bed. Then I'd go off skinny dipping in the creek..."

would come by. They'd have orchestras and folks would come in to hear them. They'd have tents and they'd come into towns like Grayson. Top flight orchestras playing for peanuts!

Were they classical?

Oh, yeah. Every now and then one of the fiddlers would break out a-playing a hoe-down. Boy, that just tickled me to death!

So you were exposed to a lot of different music?

Oh, yeah, different types of fiddle. Most of the fiddlers. I mean I did not try to copy anybody. What I did is what I feel.

You don't play like your father?

Some of my bowing is like his. I wish I had paid more attention to his bowing. He had a real smooth way of playing the fiddle. He encouraged me to use all of the bow. When I was learning, he said [the bow] was like a hacksaw. It has teeth from one end to the other. He said use it all. He said, "The way you are playing now, I could make you six fiddle bows for the one you're using." It's the truth, you know. I figured you had to jiggle it.

Now that you are retired, how much are you playing?

I think when I was working, I was playing more than I do now. But this last year I've done quite a bit of playing. I like this (the cabin jam), and they like to come in and jam. Hopefully we can keep them interested in it.

Do you think there are more fiddlers now than when you were young?

Oh, Yeah.

Why do you think that is?

Kids can learn this Suzuki method. They've got scads of them playing. I heard a story one time. Don't know if it's true, but Joe Greene and Kenny Baker was some place playing and there were some young kids there playing. Joe said, "Kenny, you ought to go over there and play something for them." Kenny said, "No, I better not, they'll play it back better than I can play it!"

J.P., without trying, you have built a name that folks know and associate with fiddling.

You know, when Annadeene and I were playing, we never tried to book places and [yet] we played about all of the major folk festivals. We were playing in Alaska and I heard this tune like nothing I ever heard before. I asked Av Gross, "What is he playing?" They said an Eskimo funeral dirge. "What's the name of it?" He said, "Ook Pik." Now I have heard all kinds of stories about that tune. A few years later, Benny Thomasson recorded that tune and now it's around everywhere.

One of the great things about your fiddling is the unexpected tunes that pop out of you every once in awhile. Like that Norwegian thing you play.

I was going through the airport in Oslo. I heard this tune. What got me was it was a pretty tune but dag gone, it must be the longest tune in the world. It just kept playing. I don't know what the name of it was. I just called it "Farewell to Norway," because I was leaving. It came in handy. I was at Old Songs Festival doing this workshop. There were these three girls there on stage, too. I didn't know what they wanted to do. They said play some fiddle tunes. These girls were playing high brow Ukrainian stuff. It was Greek to me. One gal had a Hardanger fiddle. She put a reed in her mouth and got to humming the tune and playing. She started to dance and about tore that place down. There wasn't an American tune played. So I played that Norwegian tune and they liked it real well.

Your style is so lyrical. I almost hear words.

If I play a song, I play it by the words. Sometimes a melody is enough for a tune, they just don't need much decoration.

Did anyone else in your family play fiddle?

No, sir. It was a big family — nine brothers and four sisters. There are only three of us left and I'm the only one who played fiddle. It got me out of a lot of work. You know we owned a lot of property down along the Sandy River. Daddy'd run the store. He'd put us boys out there to work. I was already playing when I was little. He had us hoeing corn. God, it was hot. I'd say, "Daddy, if I go on home, I believe I could play 'Sally Goodin.'" He said, "When you get to the end of the row there, set your hoe there and go on down and play the fiddle." My brothers were getting mad at me. They'd see me leave. I'd go down there, I'd get the fiddle out and play it about five minutes. Then I'd put it back under the bed. Then I'd go off skinny dipping in the creek. It was far away from my brothers. I'd stay there swimming until it was time for them to come in. Then I'd go back and get that fiddle and be settin' on the porch — just like I'd fiddled all day. My mother said I was gonna get caught one day. But it got me out of a lot of work.

We could hear another session starting up in the house. Figuring that we had spent enough time talking, we returned to the living room and the good music.

Discography

J.P. and Annadeene Fraley
- *Maysville* (Rounder 0351)
- *Wild Rose of the Mountain* (Rounder 0037) (currently out of stock)
- *Another Side of the Fraleys* (Road's End 001)

- *Galleynipper* (June Appal C-3919)
- Various Artists, *The Land of Yahoe: Children's Entertainments from the Days Before Television* (Rounder Kids CD 9041)

[For information about J.P.'s recordings (which may be ordered directly from him) and his occasional "Fiddlers Dream Retreat" workshops, contact Danielle Fraley, Director, Road's End Productions, P.O. Box 254, Hitchins, KY 41146.]

Maysville

Johnny Gimble:
In Full Swing!

By Jack Tuttle

Johnny Gimble has been entertaining audiences around the world for over five decades. Now 73 years old, he still displays the infectious enthusiasm for performing that has been his trademark all his career. One of the few true giants of the fiddling world, he has performed with many of the biggest names in the music industry including Bob Wills, Willie Nelson and Merle Haggard and has won two Country Music Association Instrumentalist Of The Year Awards. Gimble has long been recognized as the leader of his field — his playing has been the most studied of any fiddler in the western swing style. Gimble's solos reflect a lifelong pursuit of improvising, with endless variations that always seem the perfect embodiment of this genre.

Born in Texas in 1926, Johnny Gimble was one of nine children. Five of the boys were musically inclined and basically self-taught. Among the nine of them, the boys played guitar, fiddle, mandolin, and jug.

Could you tell me a little about how you got started?

By the time my older brothers Bill and Jack joined the Navy, we were playing some gigs, making two dollars a day playing all day Saturday for a flour company, in a cheap imitation of the Light Crust Doughboys [an early version of Bob Wills' Texas Playboys]. That's how it all started. I had an uncle John, who played a little old mandolin, he played "Washington Lee Swing" out on the front porch. And then Uncle Paul Gimble played the fiddle, had an old sorry fiddle that hung on the wall and a bad mandolin, and he played "Blue Ridge Mountain Home" and "Bully of the Town..." The live music just thrilled me, from the time I first heard it. And then, of course, recorded music thrilled me, after I heard it. So we learned kind of catch as catch can. When we did get a radio when I was ten years old, we'd listen to the Light Crust Doughboys every day. Consequently, I played a lot of tunes wrong — we picked them up as we could hear them. Then, after we got a record player, we could set the needle back and listen a little closer and learn from it.

So never in this period did you have instruction of any kind...

Well, only from other fiddlers...I guess when I was about eleven or twelve years old, my brother Bill got a record player. He traded a 45 pistol for a combination automatic record player, an old Brunswick job. I didn't realize for ten or twenty years that that thing was playing a whole tone sharp. I had a record of Bob Wills playing "Carolina in the Morning," and he did a real tricky thing on it. It was in D. I'd sit and play with it — it was real fast, but I didn't know that the record player was fast. Ten years later I was playing with Bob, and he played it in C, and at a real relaxed tempo. Anyway, that was the way we learned. When I got records of Cliff Bruner — "Draggin' the Bow" and "I'll Keep on Loving You" and those things he did in 1938...he was the number one fiddle player in the world from then on until I heard J.R. Chatwell in '43, and then there was a tie for first place. J.R. was really a jazz-swing fiddler. And that was the direction we went. We heard the Light Crust Doughboys, we heard the Shelton Brothers, with Jimmy Thomason playing fiddle.

My brothers and I had a radio show on KGKB in Tyler, Texas, when I was about thirteen. Three times a week we'd play a fifteen minute show with Gene [Gimble] and Jerry [Gimble] and myself and another boy about Gene's age named James Ivie...We had this radio show for a couple of years I guess, and then we played parties around home. When I got out of high school, I went to play with the Shelton Brothers, when I was seventeen years old, over in Shreveport [Louisiana]. KWKH radio. We played school shows and dances and a daily radio show early in the morning and then a noon show three times a week. It was really exciting for me. From there I went with Jimmy Davis when he campaigned for governor. I played tenor banjo for them. I was doubling tenor banjo and fiddle with the Shelton Brothers — The Sunshine Boys, they called their group. Then I went in the Army. Didn't get to play except for my own amusement while I was in the service. I came out and the Gimble boys reunited and we formed The Blues Rustlers and had a radio show down in South Texas and played dances...Then in '47 I went with Jesse James and the Gang at KTBC in Austin, which was the number one band in this area at that time, and from there to Corpus Christi with the Roberts Brothers Rhythmaires. These three brothers had this band and I married their niece, Barbara, and then I joined Bob Wills in '49, and the rest is geography.

*"I remember Jack [Gimble] telling me one night in '47 — we had our little band
and we were going home from a gig, and he told me, 'I was real disappointed in you
tonight.' I said, 'Why?' He said, 'You played something just like you did last night.'"*

When you were learning off of records, did you actually learn the solos?

No. We tried to play it different every time. I remember Jack [Gimble] telling me one night in '47 — we had our little band and we were going home from a gig, and he told me, "I was real disappointed in you tonight." I said, "Why?" He said, "You played something just like you did last night." So that was our aim — to never repeat. I found out when I went on the Wills band, Tiny Moore said that Bob wanted you to play all that you knew — he wanted you to knock him out and surprise him. Then at the same time we had so many lead instruments with Bob's band that you didn't get as many solos. I remember sitting next to Tiny and hearing him rehearsing with his volume off. When somebody'd be playing, he'd be sitting there going over something and then he'd play it. That was a bring-down to me. I thought everything he did was right off the cuff.

Do you still pick the fiddle up a lot and still practice?

Oh, yeah. It still amazes me. A while ago, when I was waiting for you to call, I probably wrote a tune. I don't play anything in particular. Maybe it's a breakdown, maybe it's a waltz. That's how I wrote those waltzes. I've written four or five waltzes that have a lot of double stops in them. I just fool with chords and turn a tape on. And when I'm driving to the post office, I'll punch a tape in and hear it, and say, "Well, that's a pretty good little old melody there." It's interesting to listen to yourself. The only thing wrong with that is, like you were saying a while ago, "Do you memorize things?" You get to where you play clichés of yourself. But I like to tape a dance when we play a job. And then you listen to it and amaze yourself. And it's amazing, the things Curly does on the piano. Curly has never played anything the same way once. It's new every time…That's what's good about jazz and swing.

Partial Discography (recent recordings)

Available on CD and cassette:
* *Under X in Texas,* Johnny and his band, Texas Swing
* *Playboys II,* with Herb Remington, Leon Rausch and others.
* *San Antonio Rose,* Playboys II
* *The Texas Fiddle Collection* (CMH Records CD-9027)

Available on cassette:
* *Glorybound,* Johnny Gimble & Texas Swing (Gospel instrumentals)

Instructional videos:
* *Intro To Gimble Fiddlin'*
* *Gimble's Home Aid Jam*

To order Johnny's recordings or videos, or for booking information, contact him at P.O. Box 347, Dripping Springs, TX 78620; email: bobnjon@freewwweb.com

Barefoot Fiddler

By Johnny Gimble. Transcribed by Jack Tuttle as played by Johnny Gimble on his *The Texas Fiddle Collection* album (CMH Records CD-9027).

"This tune came to me when I was sittin' around with no shoes on. Reminded me of when my uncle,
Paul Gimble, used to sit on the porch after a day in the fields and play for the kids." — Johnny Gimble

Bruce Greene: Carrying on Kentucky's Old Time Fiddle Traditions

By Mary Larsen

When Bruce Greene left his native New Jersey to study folklore at Western Kentucky University, he probably never dreamed the music he loved would become such a big part of his life. As a college student and afterwards, Bruce befriended and learned from many Kentucky fiddlers born in the last century who still played the old style. Bruce has been carrying on these archaic tunes and this lovely old style of playing ever since. His critically-acclaimed album "Five Miles of Ellum Wood: Old Time Kentucky Fiddle Solos" pays tribute to those old-timers he learned from and whom he deeply respects. Although Bruce is sad to see the traditions of the world disappearing day by day, he is certainly doing his part to carry on his own preferred style of traditional music. In addition to recording, Bruce occasionally teaches at such summer music schools as Augusta, Mars Hill, Swannanoa, and the Festival of American Fiddle Tunes.

Were the fiddlers you looked up in Kentucky open and eager to share their music and stories with you?

Well, it varied quite a bit. There were some that were still playing actively more or less, and they were glad of anybody to get together with. But then there were a lot of people, the real old guys, that quit years ago, had just kind of forgotten about it, and I had to push them a lot to get them to play. Like the first time I'd go there they wouldn't play, wouldn't play, wouldn't play, and I'd come back again a month later, they'd feel like playing that time. I think part of it was just not being sure about a stranger. So they'd wait and see if you were going to come back and weren't just somebody passing through. It varied all the time.

What are some of the differences between western and eastern Kentucky styles?

...The more I think about it over the years, the less I can distinguish styles, because the people I learned from, and the music I've heard from all around Kentucky, it's so dependent on the individual. There was one man I learned a lot from out in western Kentucky, who really played more like what people think of as an eastern Kentucky style. It's hard for me to generalize a style... Eastern Kentucky is known for having that dark, modal sounding stuff, a lot of solo playing, a lot of cross-tuning, things like that. And western Kentucky, at least when I was around there, didn't have too much of that... It was close enough to Nashville and the Grand Ole Opry and all that, I think it was influenced a lot by radio. One thing I would say is that there wasn't the kind of isolation in western Kentucky that there was in eastern Kentucky, so I think they had more influences passing through. Whereas in eastern Kentucky, there were a lot of people that really just were there and were never really affected by much outside their own region.

One thing I've thought a lot about, if you talk about Kentucky style, is I think, especially with eastern Kentucky, a lot of the style is not so much to do with that region as it is to do with being an older style. Recordings I've heard of real old fiddlers from other parts of the country seem to me very much like the eastern Kentucky style fiddlers, and that made me think that it's more something to do with how far back in time the style goes, more than what regions they're from. So what you think of as a classic eastern Kentucky style, to me is just really more of an older style that was probably a lot more widespread in the old days, and it just kind of hung on in eastern Kentucky longer. People like Marcus Martin and Bill Hensley, the old fiddlers down here in North Carolina, they could just as well have been from Kentucky, the way I knew Kentucky music. Some of the Mississippi fiddlers that people listen to, it's the same way. It's pretty vague stuff, because we have so few examples of the older players, from back in the 1800s. There are really just isolated little examples of playing from that time. So it's awful risky to make too many generalizations.

When you teach at various summer workshops, are there any specific techniques you teach?

Well, I concentrate a lot on bowing. I know a lot of unusual tunes and kind of rare tunes that people are interested in. But I do try to give them some basic bowing techniques, of what I know as kind of the older style traditional playing. I put a lot of emphasis on that, because all the older fiddlers always say that all your playing is in the bow for the old southern style stuff. And it really is pretty true for most of

> *"…What I love about fiddling are the traditions that have been handed down to us."*

the tunes. A lot of it's not near as notey as northern music, or contest style stuff, things like that. Although some of it is. But generally speaking, it's more kind of hoedown stuff, and there is a lot of bow work involved. So that's really what I like to emphasize…

A lot of a tune is defined by the certain bowing patterns that you have, and that affects the notes you make. One of the old fiddlers described it to me that you would start out with a long down pull of the bow and fill in with a lot of sawing and different kinds of patterns, shuffling kind of things, and generally you try to end up the phrase with an up stroke of the bow. Wherever you go, people have different names to describe things like that, but John Salyer's family always said that he would describe it as rolling the bow. Like to end a phrase on an up-stroke of the bow, you would come down and roll the bow back over to end up going up, and it could be done in bunch of different ways, with different kinds of shuffling patterns, but it always ended up with the bow rolling back up in an upward direction.

Do you work out the bowings for all your tunes, or does it come naturally now?

Well, it does kind of come naturally more and more. Sometimes there are certain places in a tune where I'll have to think about what will make it work best, so I do sometimes work things out that way. But generally, you just learn your own style and technique after awhile and things fall into it. For a long time I tried really hard to learn to play just like the people I learned the tunes from. As time goes on, I find the tunes are changing, the way I play them, to see myself better in the style… My style is a conglomeration of a lot of things I've learned, from a lot of different fiddlers. So if I take a tune that I learned real close to the way one of them played, eventually it sort of gets worked around to fit into the way it naturally comes to me.

You hold your fiddle against your chest or shoulder. Did you learn that way originally or did you pick it up when you went to Kentucky?

I guess I did pick it up after I went to Kentucky. And I kind of experimented back and forth with it under my chin and against my chest for quite a while, and I'm not sure why I ended up with the against the chest thing. A lot of those old people hold it that way, but not all of them. I guess I thought it looked old-timey or something, you know? [Laughter] Then I got stuck that way.

Do you have any advice for people learning?

You know, it's funny, I look at myself as kind of in a backwater or something with fiddling, because I've concentrated so much on just a certain region's music. I kind of feel like I'm a little out of the mainstream. But something I always did think a lot about was…to me, what I love about fiddling are the traditions that have been handed down to us. Everywhere you go there was a different tradition and a different style of playing, and that's what I love about music and fiddling, and I think that's partly why I've tried so much just to play one regional type of playing. Because I hate to see all the different regional styles get homogenized and disappear. I guess if I were going to give some advice, that's what I would encourage people to do: try to learn the music of a region, or a style, and learn it really well, and not try to do too many different things. I guess that attitude fits into a lot of my philosophy about life in the first place.

As time changes, especially as the older traditional fiddlers are all dying out, fiddling is really changing. People don't have their example to hold onto very much. Fiddling's becoming a lot more, I'd say eclectic, I guess. People just play whatever appeals to them, without worrying about where it came from or anything like that. In a way, I think that's really a shame, but at the same time, when I think about the old people I knew, most of them didn't have any prejudices about it like that. They learned anything they came across that they happened to like. They wouldn't say, "That doesn't sound like an old Kentucky piece, I'm not going to learn that." Anything that grabbed their attention, they'd try to learn it, because they just loved music. They weren't aware of preserving a regional style. It's hard to say. Traditional fiddling has kind of moved on into a realm of preserving something, rather than just playing what you grew up around.

Discography
- *Five Miles of Ellum Wood* (unaccompanied fiddle tunes), 1997
- *Fiddler's Dozen* (with Hilary Dirlam, guitar)
- *Vintage Fiddle Tunes* (with Hilary Dirlam, guitar)

- *Old-Time Pickin'* (Red Wilson, fiddle, and Bruce Greene, banjo)
- *Hog Went Through the Fence, Yoke and All* (Don Petty, lap dulcimer, and Bruce Greene, fiddle)

Video: *Carrying on the Traditions: Appalachian Fiddling Today* (Fiddler Magazine FMV-01)

[To contact Bruce about recordings, workshops or bookings, write him at Route 5, Box 340, Burnsville, NC 28714.]

Five Miles of Ellum Wood

Transcribed by Jack Tuttle as played by Bruce Greene on his *Five Miles of Ellum Wood* recording. *The notation is written for AEAE tuning, though on the recording the fiddle is actually tuned considerably lower.* — *Jack Tuttle.*

Duck River

From the Salyer family. Transcribed by Jack Tuttle as played by Bruce Greene on his cassette *Vintage Fiddle Tunes.*

Richard Greene: Coming Home to Bluegrass

By Jim D'Ville

Richard Greene began studying classical violin at age five. At age thirteen, he gave up the instrument, but returned while a student at U.C. Berkeley after being caught up in the old-time fiddle playing of Mike Seeger. In the early '60s, Greene, a Los Angeles native, spent time in L.A. absorbing the new acoustic music scene. During that time Greene studied the fiddle styles of Scotty Stoneman and western swing fiddler Dale Potter.

In the mid-'60s, a stint with the Greenbriar Boys led to a job with the father of bluegrass music, Bill Monroe. Greene recorded fourteen sides with Monroe between October 1966 and January 1967. Such Monroe classics as "Blue Night" and "Midnight on the Stormy Deep" came from those sessions. After leaving the Blue Grass Boys in March of 1967, Greene worked in a series of eclectic bands including the Jim Kweskin Jug Band, Seatrain with Peter Rowan, Muleskinner with Rowan, David Grisman, Clarence White, Bill Keith and Stuart Shulman, and the Great American Fiddle Band, also with Grisman, which later became the Great American Music Band.

In the '70s, Greene toured and recorded with Loggins and Messina, and concentrated on studio work. In 1977, however, Greene felt the need to resume classical violin training. His renewed interest in classical violin led him to form the Greene String Quartet in 1985 and explore such genres as jazz, blues, and rock. These days Richard Greene has returned to bluegrass in a big way, having recently released his third Rebel Records recording of bluegrass, old time, and original tunes entitled Sales Tax Toddle, and touring with his band The Grass is Greener.

I've heard it said that you were the first fiddle player to bring the symphonic sound of the violin to bluegrass when you played with Bill Monroe and the Blue Grass Boys.

Symphonic is a very general term. I think that a classical sound is a better way to put it. And to be really accurate, I would say Chubby Wise, who was Bill's first fiddler on the bluegrass recordings when the music finally tipped over from old-time to bluegrass, was the first one to do that. His sound in those days was very full, very beautiful, very well-maintained, and amazingly in tune. I don't know if he was a classically trained musician — I don't think he was. But it doesn't matter. He brought those values to bluegrass music. And that created a serious challenge for all the fiddlers that followed him — they could never have his tone. And so no fiddler between him and me had that sound; they had fiddle sound. It's a different thing. And you can't fault it — it's a beautiful, pure sound, but it doesn't have the fullness of tone that is involved in classical violin.

How is this fullness of tone achieved?

It's how you draw the bow on the string, but also choice of instrument, strings, where you sit on the mic, choice of mic, where you put the bow on the string, how fast you pull it… the classical violinist learns how to project and throw like a ventriloquist. Imagine standing in front of an eighty piece orchestra — there are no mics, the violinist has to be louder, or at least appear to be. So it's a throwing of tone.

What inspired you to form The Grass is Greener and record albums of traditional bluegrass instrumentals?

I had a need to interact and communicate more fully in a musical way than I had been doing for the last many years. As a studio musician, you are told what to play, it has nothing to do with the expression of what I've been, which is a bluegrass fiddler. I was a devout disciple of Bill Monroe when I played in the band. So when seeking out which ways I could find musical satisfaction, it dawned on me, what do people really say about me, and even though I hadn't done it for many years, I am still known as a bluegrass fiddler.

So what was your first step to get back into bluegrass?

I attended the IBMA [International Bluegrass Music Association] convention in Owensboro, Kentucky, in 1993. I had no idea what would happen. When I got there I saw all these people I hadn't seen for years who still remembered me, and I found that platform for musical communication quite quickly. It was a tidal wave of what I was looking for. It's a week of jamming in a ten story hotel. In the

"I still have Bill Monroe in the back of my head at all times because when I was in his band he was always telling me, 'This is okay, that's not,' and I still use that ethic."

atrium, where the ten stories go up, every balcony has bands playing. So you walk into this atrium and you hear fifty bands, all of them really good, playing all at once and in different keys! That sound is unforgettable.

In addition to recording and touring with The Grass is Greener, I understand you spend a lot of time researching old tunes.

I've done that since before working with Monroe — the music is just fantastic. When you find one, and you check around and find out that no one has even heard of it, let alone recorded it, it's like an exciting archaeological find. And I love to bring that music to the band. To hear David Grier, our guitarist, play "Little Rabbit" just kills me. It's such a great transposition of forces to hear the music go from the Crockett Mountaineers to David Grier and still be the same tune. It's exciting. And that music happens to be right for me, too.

How do you go about finding these tunes?

There are a handful of experts on fiddle I rely on. In fact, there are two record labels, Sierra and Rebel, who are owned by guys who began their careers by releasing fiddle music, John Delgatto and Dave Freeman. These are the guys that have collected and released it and know everything about it. In particular Dave Freeman, who is more of an archivist. Other collectors also send me tapes. I love the way I got "Northern White Clouds," for example. Someone sent me a tape of Monroe live on the Opry recorded off the radio. That's real source. "Northern White Clouds" was presented as a fiddle tune with Monroe taking one break. So I took only Monroe's break, I didn't listen to the fiddle, and notated it very precisely, and that was the source for my arrangement of the song. I defined the tune that way….

"Little Rabbit" is now a widely recorded fiddle tune. When did you first come across it?

The tune appeared on the first album Dave Freeman ever released on County Records (#501) recorded by the Crockett Mountaineers back in the '20s. Dave pressed five hundred copies, that was it. It's a rare album. So when I recorded it in the '60s, it was virtually unknown. And in the last few years that I've been around festivals, I find people are playing that tune a lot. So I enjoy taking credit for bringing that tune back.

What was your source for "The Methodist Preacher," which was the first single you released with The Grass is Greener?

I always wanted to record "The Methodist Preacher" because I learned it from Monroe. We were sitting in a hotel, or rehearsal room somewhere, with a little Wollensack tape recorder, and we played nine or ten tunes together. That was one of them, so I swear that's how it goes. It's the way I recorded it, very "Monrovian."

Bluegrass music fans have some definite ideas about what is traditional bluegrass music and what is not. How do you make that distinction?

I still have Bill Monroe in the back of my head at all times because when I was in his band he was always telling me, "This is okay, that's not," and I still use that ethic.

Partial Discography

With The Grass Is Greener:
• *The Grass Is Greener* (Rebel 1714)
• *Wolves A' Howlin'* (Rebel 1730)
• *Sales Tax Toddle* (Rebel 1737)
  (1998 Grammy nominee)

With Muleskinner (Richard Greene, Clarence White, Peter Rowan, Bill Keith, David Grisman):
• *Muleskinner* (Sierra SXCD 6009)
• *Muleskinner Live* (Sierra SXCD 6000)

With The Greene String Quartet:
• *Molly on the Shore* (Hannibal HNCD 1333)
• *The String Machine* (Virgin Classics 91632)
• *Bluegreene* (Virgin Classics 5-45133)

New Vinyl LPs:
• *Duets* (Rounder 0075)
• *Ramblin* (Rounder 0110)
• *Blue Rondo* (Sierra GA 1981)
• *Bluegrass Album: Rowan, Greene & the Red Hot Pickers* (Nippon Columbia YX-7225-N)
• *Molly on the Shore* (Hannibal 1333)

Compilation CD:
• *The Greene Fiddler* (Sierra SXCD 6005) (Previously unreleased Richard Greene originals in various band settings from rock to jazz to bluegrass)

Video:
• *Bluegrass Fiddle: A Private Lesson with Richard Greene* (Homespun Video, 800-33-TAPES/914-246-2550)

All recordings available from Richard Greene: Greener Grass Productions, 6234 Rockcliff Dr., Los Angeles, CA 90068.
(800) GRASS-93;
email: violiner@LABridge.com

This interview took place in the month of October, 1995. A lot has happened to bluegrass in the intervening three and a half years, most significantly the passing of the genre's inventor Bill Monroe, whose music is based entirely on old-time fiddle. My studies of old-time American fiddle music have continued, and I have been setting these wonderful nuggets of tunes in the string orchestra context. It is sad to observe that American fiddle music does not have enough "industry" support for its sustenance and really very few people even know of its existence. This could all change for the better if we could just find an avenue or already established genre within which to show its charm. We need a kind of American "Riverdance" phenomenon, and a little of this is starting to happen with Mark O'Connor's "country-classical-crossover" efforts. I am currently composing a piece for violin and orchestra entitled "What if Mozart Played with Bill Monroe"; the first movement is based on "Panhandle Country." I have also composed several pieces for my four-piece band and string orchestra, wherein the orchestra is actually the fifth band member, and there have been recent performances of this music by the Fiddlers' Philharmonic out of Saline, Michigan, and by the Henry Mancini Institute Orchestra here in California; the response has been terrific. I always make sure that the "legitimate" string players I work with in these groups know how to play it "right" — I don't hesitate to demonstrate for these musicians how I do it. And by the way, I have found that most classical players have no problem with the style once it's explained clearly and with the proper notation. It is my hope that through the classical world, this music will become popularized and familiar to the general public. Ironically, the bluegrass world is not supporting the idea of "fiddle music" even though the bluegrass festival scene could provide a big boost in this direction. This is especially frustrating in light of the fact that the inventor of the genre based his invention entirely on old-time fiddle music. Don't forget that I'm talking about American fiddle music — Celtic is doing just fine. So *VIVE LA FIDDLE!*

— Richard Greene, March, 1999

The Methodist Preacher

Transcribed by Richard Greene as played by Richard Greene on *The Grass Is Greener* (Rebel CD 1714). ©1995 Art and Music, BMI. Note: Only partial bowings included. [For other Richard Greene transcriptions, write: Greener Grass Productions, 6234 Rockcliff Drive, Los Angeles, CA 90068.]

John Hartford:
The Language of Fiddle Tunes

By Peter Anick

Many of us "baby boomers" remember John Hartford's appearances on the Glen Campbell TV show in the mid-sixties. The deep-voiced composer of "Gentle on My Mind" went on to become a fixture in the folk scene, combining his prolific songwriting, instrumental virtuosity and indefatigable footwork into a one-of-a-kind one man show that cheerfully bridged the gap between old and new. John first got his inspiration to play the fiddle as a young boy in Missouri; his parents took him to square dances with them where there was often live fiddle music. He then began teaching himself to play by sneaking his grandfather's fiddle out from its hiding place in a closet and practicing on the sly. On how he decided to become a professional musician, John says, "I didn't decide. It just kinda took me over. I was originally going to be a riverboat pilot. Music was my second choice, and it just wouldn't let me alone..." A self-described "chronic improvisor," John counts among his major fiddling influences Gene Goforth, Benny Martin, Ed Haley, Dr. Jimmy Gray, Texas Shorty, Benny Thomasson, and Major Franklin.

This past summer, as John was finishing up a songwriting workshop at the Winterhawk Bluegrass Festival, I asked him if he would share some thoughts about writing fiddle tunes. He suggested that we actually try composing a tune and we retired to his bus to do just that. In this interview, John intersperses his composing with his insights on a whole range of fiddlistic topics.

Photo: David Schenk

How would you compare writing a song to writing a fiddle tune?

Well, writing a fiddle tune is just writing a melody, and there are songs that are fiddle tunes, or of course you can play any song as a fiddle tune, I guess. About the same kinds of things apply. I jot 'em down as they come into my head. A lot of times, I wake up in the morning, I got something on my mind, or I can just start writing, put something down and see what comes out.

Do you have a particular goal in mind when you write a fiddle tune?

I guess I'm always trying to write "the fiddle tune," "the melody." And I don't want it to be too complicated. I just want it to be something that's memorable. The whole study of fiddle tunes and melodies and everything really probably boils down to why you like one melody over another, which is of course the 64 dollar question… Sometimes I'll be working on a melody and say, "There's no way anybody could like this." I'll change one note in it or something, and then I'll fall in love with it. Or I'll think, "Oh this is the greatest melody I ever heard," and then I'll go to play it and it won't be worth a dime…

Do you find it harder to come up with a second part than a first part?

No... [Picks up his pen.] Let's just write a tune here. This part of it I don't understand. It's just like I turn a switch and let's just see where it goes. [Hums and writes. Rearranges the bar lines.] That seems to be a pickup there, which just makes it even more interesting... [Hums it again.] What's the date today? I always date everything. Let's call this "Fiddler Magazine." That's a good title for it. I always give everything a title if I possibly can — just give it something to hang it on. [Picks up his fiddle.] All right, here's the first part. [Plays.]

Why that's only six bars! That even makes it more interesting. [Plays it again.] Yeah, I like that. Let's just make up a bridge. [Hums and writes.] I've got enough of this in my head that it'll kinda echo... [Hums.] This will kinda pull you back into that first part but it will also make us want to put a third part to it. Now this might be a little hard to play, but I'm not going to censor myself right now on that. [Plays what he has written.]

*"An exercise that I really love to do is take a tune that doesn't have a
whole lot of parts and just start making up parts as I go, just playing
it as if it had a whole bunch of parts..."*

Now you can write that all out in 16ths like that and make a tune where if you make a little mistake or something like that, it becomes something else or you have a train wreck. A lot of times I try to write tunes in a real simple style and not use as many 16ths unless I just absolutely need it to describe the contour of the melody, so that it gives me more ad libbing room... And a lot of times what I'll do is, if I start liking a tune like that, playing with it, I'll kind of get it under my fingers and play it for a while away from the paper until it starts to make sense to me. And then I'll sit back down and rewrite from memory. 'Cause I think a lot of these old tunes have been polished and repolished by countless people playing them and the good notes and the good runs survive and the ones that aren't so good....

Kind of an evolutionary selection. Listening to that tune, the first part has got a nice flow to it. It caught me by surprise that it was only six measures.

Yeah, I never know. I've had several tunes come out where the measures were weird but they made sense and when I tried to add measures to them, they didn't, so I just leave 'em in there. [Plays it over several times.] Now just for kicks... [Writes.] Now let's just reduce that down. [Plays it simplified, then fills in the holes with some ad libs, makes some changes.] There, that kind of ties it in — makes it kinda rhyme. 'Cause sometimes phrases almost need to rhyme. Now, as I play that, I could be smoothing it out. [Plays.]

What do you consider the "language" of fiddle tunes?

Boy, that'd be real hard to say! It's like Clifford Hawthorne — an old boy I grew up with — he used to say, "I may not be the best fiddler you ever heard, but, by God, I can tell when one's a bein' played!" I don't know how to tell you that. I can just listen to one and tell whether it's in the ball park or not. Benny Thomasson and Mark O'Connor are wonderful improvisors, and it's all in the fiddle tune language. The improvs almost sound like they were engraved in stone.

An exercise that I really love to do is take a tune that doesn't have a whole lot of parts and just start making up parts as I go, just playing it as if it had a whole bunch of parts... I think the one thing that helps in improvising is to always try to play in time, even when you're working something out, try to keep it going and try to keep it in time. Don't stop and noodle it out, or do that as little as possible, because then if you don't hit something, something else will come out. It'll be okay. And then the next time around, you can go for the thing again, and if it doesn't work, you've got something else.

I've done all kinds of things like write [tunes] upside down and see if I can make heads or tails of 'em or write 'em without any time and then go back and do it or take another melody and write it every other note — just crazy stuff, just to see what kind of a direction I can pull myself in if I can get some kind of a start and then take off and see where it's gonna take me.

Has that helped?

Yeah, it's been fun. Most of the best melodies are things I wake up in the morning with. I'll wake up and the whole tune'll be in my head. It's just a matter of writing it down.

If you get distracted, then, do you lose it?

Yeah, or if somebody turns on a radio or starts playing an instrument and gets another tune going, it'll wipe it out, yeah. That's suicide to do that around me in the morning! If I come down and I've got that blank look in my face and somebody turns the radio on, boy, they're usually in for some trouble!

Have you done some historical research on tracking tunes back?

I sure have. Well, I read through these old tune books and every time I find a tune that sounds like something else, I try to figure out what it is and then I make a notation on a 3X5 card and drop it in the card file. I love the fiddle tunes of the Big Sandy River Valley [between Kentucky and West Virginia] and I like the tunes from back home in Missouri, and I like the stuff in Texas and when I hear one, I try to figure out where it's from and what it's like...The study of fiddle tunes is a whole lot like studying words. If you read the Oxford dictionary and it starts talking about the history of words, it talks about it in terms of where was the first time this word was published, or where was the first time that we heard this word...So I kinda put that to fiddle tunes, too...

Do you think there are certain major fiddle players that might have contributed a large number of tunes to the "traditional" repertoire we play now?

Oh sure. Absolutely. [Shows me the book *The Rantin' Pipe and Tremblin' String* by George Emmerson, 1971.] I've read it twice and I'm a gettin' ready to read it again. I would say in the 18th century and the 19th century that we're looking at the Gow family — several generations of great fiddle players in Scotland; William Marshall in Scotland; Peter Milnes... Of course, O'Carolan — we're still finding stuff of his. These guys were prolific. They wrote volumes of stuff, and half of what they wrote, we don't even know they wrote it and we're playing it!... In the old days, it was not fashionable to say "I wrote that." The old timers would write 'em and then they'd take 'em out and play 'em and they'd say, "Here's an old tune I remember my grandfather playing." They would never own up to making it up themselves... I think it has a lot to do with the fact that they want that tune to be an "old time" tune. This business of memory in music, and this business of "old time" and it going back seems to be very important. In other words, the words "old time" — I think you'd be real hard-pressed to get that divorced from the word fiddling. Does that make sense? And so many fiddle sessions, old men like to come to fiddle sessions and listen and say, "Yup. That's the way that's supposed to go. By God, now that's the old time way of playing that, son!" I grew up with that. It was all old time and fantasizing about, "God, wouldn't you have loved to hear grandpa play that! Wouldn't you like to hear old so-and-so, wish he was still around. Boy, he could tear that thing up!"....

The whole study is what survives and why. Some tunes, the reason they hang around is because they are hard to play and they become competitive pieces. Scotty Fitzgerald, he played a tune [plays], which is "Acrobat's Hornpipe." And that's in Bb and it's got a lot of fingering to it and everything like that. It's not an ironclad tune, necessarily, but it's got a lot of stuff on it so that it can be competitive. It's like, "All right, let's see you play this!" and it makes a good contest piece. A lot of fiddling is competitive. It's centered around contests, who can beat who, and that is part of its beauty. To a fiddler, that's beautiful.

What exactly is your definition of an "ironclad" tune?

Well, it's any tune, to me, that anybody can play and mess up pretty bad and it'll still be that tune. As opposed to a tune where, if somebody messes it up, it either becomes something else or it just falls apart. [Demonstrates by playing "Old Joe Clark" a dozen very different ways.] Now the core of "Old Joe Clark" is just [plays], so all those rhythmic hooks and everything like that, I can take any one of those tunes and start dressing it up with rhythmic hooks, you know. And also, too, the way you play has a lot to do with it. One guy can take a melody and it's just, "Hmmm. I don't see anything in that," and the next guy can play the exact same notes and you go, "God, do I love that!"

[Some months later, we continued the interview by phone. John has reworked his "Fiddler Magazine" tune a bit, extending the 6 measure sections to 8 measures and adding another part.]

That last part, it just occurred to me it needed a part where the notes "dwelled" a little bit. It's kind of a ragtime thing, and also I like it when a fiddle tune has a part in there that kinda sounds like it's the tune and then kinda sounds like somebody stole it out of an old song.

Are there any places where you think a specific bowing ought to be notated?

Not really, 'cause I don't really think of bowing that way. Maybe I should, but I kinda improvise the bowing as I go along, and I try to change it up, of course. I kind of agree with Mark O'Connor about not keeping the same pattern any longer than about two bars. And I'll play long bow and then I'll play two and three notes per stroke and then I'll play some of that off string bowing, and then two and one one, you know yah, dah dah, yah. I play a little bit of that sometimes. Of course, a lot of times, after you get a handle on the melody, which is like a joke — it's like getting a joke — once you get a handle on the melody, you're liable not to play it exactly note for note the same way every time you go through it, so then your bowing will probably change anyway.

How would you categorize the style of the "Fiddler Magazine" tune?

Oh, I don't know if I would. It just came out of my head. And what's in my head is all the influences I've ever had, all the way back to growing up with Dr. Gray and Gene Goforth, and people I played with when I was young.... I hear a lot of music and then I go off and the music starts recombining itself in my head and I guess that's the improvising. I can remember the tunes, but then the tunes all go together and start marrying each other and producing new tunes in my head, and I don't know where it comes from. That's probably the part of what I am and what I do that I understand the least. It's like there's a valve in there and I turn the valve and all this stuff comes out.

Discography

Albums

- *The Speed of the Old Long Bow (A Tribute to the Fiddle Music of Ed Haley)* (Rounder, 1998)
- *The Bullies Have All Gone to Rest* (Jim Wood, fiddle, & John Hartford, banjo) (Whippoorwill Records, 1998)
- *Wild Hog In the Red Brush* (Rounder, 1996) (Grammy nominee)
- *No End of Love* (Small Dog A-Barkin)
- *The Fun of Open Discussion* (with Bob Carlin (Rounder, 1995)
- *Live at College Station, PA* (Small Dog A-Barkin, 1994)
- *Old Sport* (with Texas Shorty on fiddle) (Small Dog A-Barkin, 1994)
- *The Walls We Bounce Off Of* (Small Dog A-Barkin, 1994)

- *Goin' Back to Dixie* (Small Dog A-Barkin, 1992)
- *Cadillac Rag* (with Mark Howard) (Small Dog A-Barkin, 1991)
- *Hartford and Hartford* (Flying Fish, 1991)
- *Down on the River* (Flying Fish, 1989)
- *Me Oh My, How the Time Does Fly* (Rounder, 1987)
- *Annual Waltz* (MCA Dot, 1987)
- *Clements, Hartford, Holland* (Rounder, 1995, 1984)
- *Dillard/Hartford/Dillard* (Flying Fish, 1995, 1980, 1977)
- *Nobody Knows What You Do* (Flying Fish, 1992, 1976)
- *Mark Twang* (Flying Fish, 1989, 1976)
- *Morning Bugle* (Rounder, 1995, prev. Warner Bros., 1972)
- *Aereo-Plain* (Rounder, 1997, 1971)

- *Catalogue* (Flying Fish, 1984)
- *Gum Tree Canoe* (Flying Fish/County Line)

Videos:
- *John Hartford's Old Time Fiddling (Trying to teach my hands to do what I hear in my head)* (Fiddler Magazine FMV-05, 1997)
- *Banjoes, Fiddles & Riverboats: John Hartford and the General Jackson* (avail. from Small Dog A-Barkin)

Small Dog A-Barkin is John's own recording company. Small Dog A-Barkin recordings, as well as most of the other titles, may be ordered directly from John at P.O. Box 443, Madison, TN 37116; http://www.techpublishing.com/hartford/

For bookings, contact Keith Case & Associates, (615) 327-4646.

In my mind when I wrote this tune, I imagined the great Fiddler Magazine Building with its bright flashing orange neon "FIDDLER" sign on top, twelve floors (one for each note in the chromatic scale), and the editor's private helicopter pad on the roof. And I could see Mike, Chris, Bob, and myself trying to get in, dealing with one of the many receptionists, failing to produce the right photo IDs, and the burly uniformed guard showing us right back out into the parking lot. Then, with Bob leading the way, finally getting back in through another large double glass door into a world of marble floors, walls, and statuary, and an incredible array of sophisticated electronics arranged in huge office areas humming with industrial strength activity. Signs everywhere, "Bowing Department," "The Bureau of Rosin and Strings," "This way to Breakdowns and Reels," "Tailpiece Division," and "The Hornpipe Desk." And then, again we're discovered and ushered out through "The Broken Bridge and Used String Repository" through two large overhead garage doors, off the loading dock and back out into the parking lot. Looking up, I could almost feel the incredible activity on the upper ten floors — the great notation studio where artists and calligraphers labor to make the beautiful tune transcriptions, the endless library of photos — and all the suites of plush offices devoted to the different styles: Texas, New England, Upper Midwest, Missouri, Cajun, Eastern Kentucky, North Carolina, Tennessee, Mississippi, Alabama, and on and on like musical embassies defining the great fiddle techniques and helping them to get along with one another. Oh Glory, to think, a beautiful magazine for the lowly fiddler, the common violinist! For this I offer my humble tune. — John Hartford

Fiddler Magazine

By JohnHartford, ©John Hartford Music, BMI

Ivan Hicks:
Maritime Musical Ambassador

By Paulette Webb

In 1946, Ivan Hicks was just getting his first lessons in how to play for an old time square dance. With the dance floor full and his father at his side, Ivan soon developed the art of playing for dancers. Ivan has often recounted his father's words of advice: "Just pick out a couple who are good dancers, watch them and play to them." As time moved on, Ivan's father's job kept him from playing, so Ivan moved into Curtis Hicks' seat and played for hundreds of dances.

Ivan went on to become a member of various bands playing styles of music other than old time fiddling. In the 1950s, the Golden Valley Boys were doing radio shows, playing concerts and recording old time and country music. From 1969 to 1989, Ivan could be found traveling around the Maritimes with Marshwinds, a popular dance band that specialized in country, rock and roll, and a few fiddle tunes for good measure. Ivan was the guitar player and lead vocalist for Marshwinds. In the late '70s, Ivan's interest in doing a recording of old time fiddling prompted the formation of the old time and bluegrass group Maritime Express. Ivan and Maritime Express recorded many albums over the years featuring old time fiddling, bluegrass and gospel. They travelled extensively in the Maritimes, Ontario, and performed for several years in New York State.

It seemed that fiddling was taking a back seat to these other kinds of music and although Ivan was playing country, rock and roll, and bluegrass music, he never lost sight of his fiddle. He recognized the need for old time fiddle music to be preserved and promoted, and one way he could contribute would be to teach. In the late '70s, he began teaching children and adults the art of fiddling. Ivan has shared his talents with many students, young and old alike, and has been an inspiration to countless others. One can see the pride in his smile as he listens to the young student fiddlers play. He is equally happy to be in the company of the Sussex Avenue Fiddlers, a group of adults who meet at Ivan and his wife Vivian's home for instruction and practice and to prepare for the next performance somewhere in the Maritimes.

For his tireless efforts in the promotion and preservation of fiddle music, Ivan has been awarded many honors. In 1985, he was inducted into the New Brunswick Country Music Hall of Fame, and in 1990 into the North American Fiddlers Hall of Fame. Ivan and Vivian were the first recipients of the beautiful Tara Lynne Memorial Award which was presented by the Maritime Fiddlers Association at the 1995 Maritime Old Time Fiddling Contest in Dartmouth, Nova Scotia. The list of awards is a long one and is a testament to Ivan's love for old time fiddling. In an article called "The Master Fiddler," written by Wayne Harrigan of *That Riverview Magazine,* the author describes Ivan as being "...synonymous with the type of music which is part of Atlantic Canada's heritage." Ivan has become a great musical ambassador for the Maritimes, its music, and its musicians.

Even though Ivan had a full schedule with his job as a high school science teacher, he found time to be a solid supporter of old time music in many different ways. He hosted a weekly fiddle show, "Fiddling 30," on radio station CFQM for thirteen years; made many appearances on television, at festivals, concerts, fairs, benefits, seniors' homes; competed in and won many fiddling contests; acted as MC at numerous events including the Maritime Fiddling Contest in Dartmouth, Nova Scotia, and at the Canadian Old Time Fiddling contest in Shelburne, Ontario; continued to compose new tunes and published a book including his compositions and some tunes played by his father; was and still is director of several fiddle associations, both Canadian and American; promoted, organized and instructed at many fiddle workshops; organized many fiddle concerts and tours; recorded an album in Nashville, Tennessee, with Maritime fiddlers Keith Ross and Bill Guest; and continues to attend as many events as time allows.

Since his retirement from public school teaching in 1996, Ivan is finding the time to move in some new directions with his music. Some of his recent activities include: establishing the Ivan Hicks Downeast Fiddle Camp in Moncton, New Brunswick; performances across Canada and into the United States; the release of a book, *Fifty Years of Fabulous Fiddling,* written by Maritime author Dr. Allison Mitcham; an excursion to Nictau, New Brunswick, each June, where "Fiddles on the Tobique" brings fiddlers and fiddling folk together in canoes to fiddle their way down the beautiful Tobique River; and the organization of "Fiddles of the World," a huge fiddle festival in Halifax, Nova Scotia, in July, 1999, featuring performances by fiddlers from various regions of the U.S. and Canada, the British Isles, Scandinavia, and more, as well as seminars, workshops, jams, and a trade show. Perhaps Ivan's greatest dream is to see the foundation of a music center that would feature the music and the accomplishments of musicians throughout Atlantic Canada.

Ivan had a gift and shared it. He had a vision and the will to seek it. His dedication to the music he loves has brought him many rewards, not the least of which are the smiles of happiness he sees when he plays "Maple Sugar" or "Big John McNeil" one more time!

"Ivan has become a great musical ambassador for the Maritimes, its music, and its musicians… Perhaps Ivan's greatest dream is to see the foundation of a music center that would feature the music and the accomplishments of musicians throughout Atlantic Canada."

Discography

- *The Strength of God's Hand* (gospel, instrumental/vocal)
- *Ivan Hicks and the Sussex Avenue Fiddlers' 20th Anniversary*
- *Shingle the Roof*
- *Old Time Christmas With Friends*

- *Fiddlingly Yours*
- *Swingin' Fiddles* (w. Bill Guest & Keith Ross)
- *Purple Violet Fiddling*
- *Friendly Fiddling the Maritime Way*
- *Swingin' Fiddles in Nashville*
- *Fiddling for Fun and Friends*
- *For You (Vocal)*

Video: *The Life and Music of Ivan & Vivian Hicks* (45 min.)

Book: *Fiddle Tunes & Souvenirs* (Ivan Hicks)

For information on recordings and the Ivan Hicks Downeast Fiddle Camp, contact Ivan Hicks, 157 Sussex Avenue, Riverview, New Brunswick, Canada E1B 3A8; (506) 386-2996; email: hicksi@nb.sympatico.ca.

Jim, The Fiddle Maker

Composed by Ivan Hicks, © 1980. Transcribed by Bill Guest. Played on Ivan Hicks' *Friendly Fiddling the Maritime Way* cassette.

"This tune was composed for Jim MacCleave, the violin maker from Oxford, Nova Scotia. I own two of his fiddles." — Ivan Hicks

Jerry Holland:
Cape Breton's Master Fiddler and Composer

By Mary Larsen

Jerry Holland, born and raised in Brockton, Massachusetts, has spent more than twenty years enjoying the fresh air and peacefulness of Cape Breton, an island off the northeast end of Nova Scotia. His father was from New Brunswick, and his mother was from Quebec. He had no relatives on the island, but had spent some family vacations there as a boy. Jerry explains, "It was the music, the people, and the way of life that drew me there."

At age five, Jerry began learning to play the fiddle from his father, who patiently taught him a note at a time. Of his father's fiddling, Jerry says, "He was an all-around player, but because he was a family man and a lot of the fiddlers that were in the limelight were able to travel, he wasn't well known. Anyway, he was a real nice fiddler with his own style — a combination of Don Messer, Irish, and Cape Breton music."

His father exposed Jerry to a great deal of fiddling of all styles, particularly the Cape Breton style — at house parties, on records, and at dances throughout the Boston area. Thus, by an early age, Jerry had heard such notable fiddlers as Winston "Scotty" Fitzgerald, Angus Chisholm, Bill Lamey, Johnny Wilmot, Theresa MacLellan, and many others. As Jerry says in the liner notes of his 1999 album, *Fiddler's Choice,* "I owe a great debt of gratitude to these fathers and mothers of Cape Breton music." Jerry went on to explain, "Not only did they teach music to me but they helped stimulate my interest in this music throughout my teen years. Their generosity with their wealth of music has been a great example to me. It's through this sharing of music that the tradition will continue."

Jerry's first television appearance was at the age of seven when he first stepdanced on "Don Messer's Jubilee," a variety show that aired in Canada from 1959 to 1969. It was his father who taught him to dance as well as to play the fiddle. "He got me started, and I continued on with it. Years later, I put the two of them together and played and danced at the same time. I guess you could say that was my claim to fame. Today I tell people I used to dance about 150 pounds ago. I probably danced more in my life as a young person than I'll ever play the fiddle." A multi-instrumentalist, Jerry also plays guitar, piano, mandolin, and bass guitar.

Since his early debut, Jerry has performed live, as well as on television and radio, throughout the U.S., Canada, and in several European countries. He has also performed with Angus Chisholm, Bill Lamey, Winston Fitzgerald, Joe Cormier, John Allen Cameron, and The Cape Breton Symphony.

A prolific composer (many of his tunes are compiled in *Jerry Holland's Collection of Fiddle Tunes,* Cranford Publications), Jerry's tunes have been performed by such respected Cape Breton artists as The Barra MacNeils, Howie MacDonald, Natalie MacMaster, Buddy MacMaster, The Rankin Family, and The Cape Breton Symphony, to name a few, and such international artists as Altan, Frankie Gavin, Stéphane Grappelli, Kevin Burke, Alasdair Fraser, and Barbara MacDonald Magone. Jerry's tunes have also become well-loved standards played by musicians around the world.

Jerry says, "A phrase will sometimes come very easily. I can end up with a tune in two or three minutes. The longest one took me three years. It's a tune I named for my mother, and it's kind of an ironic story. In April 1995, I had been carrying part of a tune around for three years. On April 7th, I came up with a second part for it, but I wasn't really comfortable with playing it. I worked on it that evening and finished it the next evening. I was away from home at the time. I got home the morning of April 9th, and received a message that my mother had died the night before. Shortly after her death, a lady asked me what I called the tune I had just played, and I replied, 'The tune hasn't a fitting title as yet. I composed it for my dear mother.' The lady said, 'That's it. Simply call it, For My Mother Dear.' I responded, 'That's perfect.'"

"I played it at her funeral, and I sincerely believe that it was the very best I'll ever play that tune no matter how hard I'll ever try. I'm sure that it was my mom's inspiration that made it easy for me to play it that day under such difficult circumstances. So it's a memorable piece of music for me." [The tune is on Jerry's latest recording, *Fiddler's Choice,* on the Odyssey Records label.]

When I spoke with Jerry, he was visiting and performing in the Boston area. I asked him about his previous night, and he responded, "It was a small concert in the area where I was born and brought up, and it's great to be home. Last night's concert was almost a sold-out

(Text continued on page 54.)

Boo Baby's Lullaby

By Jerry Holland. Transcribed by Paul Cranford as played on Jerry's *Fiddler's Choice* recording (Odyssey Records).
"I composed this lullaby for a very special little lady just after her birth in January 1996.
Later the next year I recorded it on the Fiddler Magazine video." — Jerry Holland

Angus MacIsaac's Jig

By Jerry Holland. Transcribed by Paul Cranford as played on Jerry's *Fiddler's Choice* recording (Odyssey Records).
"Angus MacIsaac's Jig is named after a great friend and supporter of my music." — Jerry Holland

Alexander William MacDonnell's Jig

By Jerry Holland. Transcribed by Paul Cranford as played on Jerry's *Fiddler's Choice* recording (Odyssey Records).
"Alexander William MacDonnell's Jig was composed in memory of a very special friend whom I miss dearly." — Jerry Holland

John Morris Rankin's Jig

By Jerry Holland. Transcribed by Paul Cranford as played on Jerry's *Fiddler's Choice* recording (Odyssey Records).
"John Morris Rankin's Jig is named after the fiddler, composer, piano player, and member of the well-known Cape Breton group, The Rankin Family. I always enjoy playing with John Morris… Alex William MacDonnell was John Morris' father-in-law." — Jerry Holland

> *"My father said... 'Take all the fiddlers that appeal to you, and take the best from each one. Put it together with what you like yourself, and make your own style.'"*

crowd, even with the extreme bad weather. It was wonderful. It was the first time in my professional life that I've played here in my hometown. I performed in little talent shows as a ten and eleven-year-old, thirty-plus years ago, and that was the extent of it. At the time, I tried to keep quiet about those performances because I was going to school, and I didn't want the ridicule that a fellow would have had to endure. So a lot of those events didn't get publicly announced, on my part, anyway."

I asked Jerry if there was one particular musical experience that stood out for him. He explained, "In one sense, to mention one without mentioning others wouldn't really be fair. Just playing for some of my father's old friends brought back memories for them, as well as to me. I've known these folks all my life. To experience the happiness that it brought them and the fond memories shared by all is what playing music is all about. It was really good, playing for them at the concert, as well as the home setting [in a session the night before]."

"I've played prestigious places like the Smithsonian and overseas in different settings. There was a concert in Paris that aired on Radio France. That concert was heard in thirteen countries. That was memorable too. I'm a happy person to have had the nice experiences that I've had. I find it personally rewarding to play music and to see people enjoying it."

I asked Jerry if he had any advice for fiddlers interested in learning the Cape Breton style. Jerry offered, "Cape Breton music is a very personal thing where there are no two fiddlers that sound exactly the same. There may be one hero a person will direct their attention to and want to sound like, but there's the individual aspect of the thing. Winston Fitzgerald said to me, 'There's already one Winston. There's no need for another one — create your own style.' My father said a similar thing: 'Take all the fiddlers that appeal to you, and take the best from each one. Put it together with what you like yourself, and make your own style.'"

Discography

As Featured Artist:
- *Jerry Holland* — 1976 LP; Rounder Records
- *Master Cape Breton Fiddler* — 1982 LP; Boot Records
- *Lively Steps* — 1987 cassette; Fiddlesticks Music
- *Jerry Holland Solo* — 1988 cassette; Cranford Publications
- *A Session with Jerry Holland* — 1990 cassette; Fiddlesticks Music
- *Fathers and Sons* — 1992 cassette; Fiddlesticks Music
- *The Fiddlesticks Collection* — 1995 CD & cassette; Green Linnet Records
- *Fiddler's Choice* — 1999 CD & cassette; Odyssey Records

As Guest Artist:
- *Fiddle, The Cape Breton Symphony* — 1976 LP; Glencoe Records
- *Festival of American Fiddle Tunes* — various artists; 1979 LP; Voyager Records
- *The Rise & Follies of Cape Breton* — various artists; 1981 LP; U.C.C.B. Press
- *Cape Breton's Greatest Hits* — various artists; 1981 LP; U.C.C.B. Press
- *Music from The Simon Fraser Collection* — various artists; 1982 cassette; Cranford Publications
- *Down Home with Aly Bain* — various artists; 1986 LP; Lismore Records
- *A Tribute to Dan R. MacDonald* — various artists; 1989 cassette; Cranford Publications
- *Staying in Tune* — Dougie MacDonald; 1990 cassette; a Dougie MacDonald production
- *Cape Breton Island* — various artists; 1993 CD & cassette; Nimbus Records
- *The Island* — Kenzie MacNeil; 1992 CD & cassette; a Kenzie MacNeil production
- *Open the Door* — P. MacNeil/J. MacInnis; 1992 CD & cassette; Gigs & Reel Productions
- *House Party* — Máire O'Keeffe; 1994 CD; Gael Linn Records
- *Stepping on the Bridge* — Hamish Moore; 1994 CD; Greentrax Records
- *Atlantic Fiddles* — various artists; 1994 CD; Atlantica/EMI
- *Lantern Burn* — Rita & Mary Rankin; 1994 CD; Unity Gain
- *In Jig Time* — Brenda Stubbert; 1995 CD & cassette; Stubbert Music
- *Jura Ceildh Band* — 1997 CD; Lochshore, KRL
- *The Road Home* — compilation; 1997 CD; 1997 Celtic Colours International Festival; Stephen MacDonald Productions
- *The Bridges of Cape Breton County(s)* — compilation; 1997 CD; Celestial Entertainment
- *The Cape Breton Connection* — compilation; 1997 CD; Stephen MacDonald Productions
- *Dougie MacDonald, A Miner* — Dougie MacDonald; 1998 CD & cassette; A Miner Productions
- *Fiddling Around Down North* — Joe Doucette; 1998 CD; Joe Doucette
- *The Second Wave* — compilation; 1998 CD; 1998 Celtic Colors International Festival; Stephen MacDonald Productions

Videos:
- *Cape Breton Seasons* — 1992; Dongael Video Productions
- *Carrying on the Traditions, Cape Breton Fiddling Today* — 1996; Fiddler Magazine

Interviews:
The Cape Breton Fiddler — 1982; U.C.C.B. Press
Cape Breton's Magazine — 1986; Issue 48

Books:
Jerry Holland's Collection of Fiddle Tunes — 1988, 1992, 1995; Cranford Publications

Miscellaneous:

For information on Jerry's recordings, his tour schedule, or to download some of his sheet music on .gif files, see Jerry's web site at: www.capebretonet.com/Music/Holland/ Mailing address: General Delivery, Inverness, Nova Scotia, Canada B0E 1N0; Email: jholland@ns.sympatico.ca

Books and recordings:
Cranford Publications, Box 42, Englishtown, Nova Scotia, Canada B0C 1H0; 902-929-2811; Email: psc@cranfordpub.com Web site: www.cranfordpub.com

Record company:
Odyssey Records, 125 S. Wacker Drive, Suite 300, Chicago, IL 60606-4402; 312-214-2525; Web site: www.odysseyrecords.com

Management & Booking:
Jones & Co., 1512 Sackville St., Suite 100, Halifax, Nova Scotia, Canada B3K 1K6; 902-429-9005; Email: SheriJones@compuserve.com

Väsen's Nyckelharpa Virtuoso Olov Johansson

By Matt Fichtenbaum

Photo: Thomas Fahlander

Mention nyckelharpa and people think directly of Väsen, the Swedish trio-turned-quartet whose brilliant playing and exciting mix of traditional and new material have given this instrument and Swedish music a world presence. U.S. label Northside Records has recently released two Väsen CDs and one by nyckelharpist Olov Johansson, so their music is suddenly very available and relevant in North America. This presented a perfect chance to catch up with Olov, whom I had first met in 1996, when Väsen were on staff at Scandinavian Week in Maryland, and hear about his musical origins, his thoughts on playing and teaching, life with Väsen, and any other wisdom he might share.

Väsen's sound is tight and exciting, a close blend of different players and instruments clearly with common feelings to express. Their interactions and communication while playing are striking, and they appear to be having great fun, up on stage or in the middle of the floor surrounded by dancers. I asked Olov about ensemble playing, what it takes for Väsen to play together well and what advice he might have for other players.

Olov: Väsen have played together a long time, and we had a solid common base to stand on even when we started. We have a common groove, and in it we have different tasks. You need good ears and a desire to build something that is greater than your own individual playing. You need to listen a lot to each other. Practice leading and following, practice playing exactly like your friends and take turns being the leader. When I play with someone new, I'm cautious at first; if I play the accompaniment I'll just follow along until I understand how to contribute so it helps rather than our just getting in each other's way. Once we understand each other's mindset and interpretation we can work together and make something that builds on what we both bring to it. For me it's normal to work with Roger [Tallroth, guitar], Mikael [Marin, viola], and André [Ferrari, percussion], and it's great. We all bring our different personalities and possibilities into Väsen and there we create something new and whole together.

But are you really having as much fun as it appears?

Yes, that's true. We try to do things in the music that surprise ourselves and the others in the band and that keeps it interesting and fun.

Väsen's newest recording is Whirled. *All the tunes on it are original, composed (the Swedes say "made") by the musicians themselves and presented in very contemporary style. It's irresistible to look at the development of Väsen's music since the first recording, called simply* Väsen, *released in 1990. That was entirely traditional tunes, played with great energy and superb musicianship but in a style still close to traditional. I asked Olov about the paths the group has taken since its beginnings, and he skillfully put the answer into perspective.*

First a few things about tradition. All traditional musicians throughout history whom people speak about have been innovators. They have composed new great tunes, developed a new variant of an old instrument, etc. The ones who have mostly passed a tradition on from some great fiddler aren't much remembered; it's more interesting to talk about the fiddler they themselves learned from. All the old fiddlers I have learned from have been innovators in one way or another.

The first CDs we recorded were rather faithful to the tradition but even then there were some who said there was too much new stuff in the music, while some said it was revolutionary and great. Today many say the first Väsen recording is very traditional. There are people with a narrow view of tradition and people with a wider view. I think musicians have always done what they feel like and that is also based on the tradition they have. We decided for *Whirled* that we would only play our own compositions. There is a wide range of music that comes from all four of us. But together we shape it to Väsen music.

Storsvarten is Olov's new individual recording, a fine mix of Olov's own tunes and traditional material, plus one by modern nyckelharpa master Eric Sahlström (1912-1986). Väsen's earlier recordings also prominently feature Olov's tunes, which to this listener call to mind the music that was played on the earlier, diatonic forms of nyckelharpa. I asked him about his compositions.

I don't know what it is that inspires me to make tunes. Sometimes I have experienced something that puts me in a mood to "make a new tune." Sometimes when I am sitting playing, something comes up and there we are. Sometimes I decide consciously to compose a tune and that is usually the most effective method. It's mostly after the tune is complete that I understand where I got it from. When I compose on the [older] kontrabasharpa it becomes old music automatically. The same goes for the new [nyckelharpa] in some keys.

"The image I had from home of playing music was my mother and her sisters and brothers playing together at their family parties, jamming popular songs from when they were young, and dance tunes that my grandfather used to play."

Two new recordings — one with the group and all original material, one a mix of material and an individual effort at heart — to my ear they're a delight. I asked Olov whether he agreed.

We are very happy about how *Whirled* turned out. We decided to play only our own material and that forced us to go further with our music. It was so inspiring to work as hard as we did before and during the recording. And it was our first recording effort with André, with Väsen as a quartet rather than a trio. A change like that makes for a whole new group with new dynamics, in both the musical balance and the personal and social balance. André fit right in and gave new possibilities to all aspects of the group's work.

Storsvarten was a pure pleasure to record. I searched in my mind for old tunes and I composed new ones. I started to practice and play at home more than ever because of this recording. I chose to play together with some of the people I most enjoy playing with. I also longed to play more traditional material since we don't play so much of that in Väsen anymore. I wanted to record it in a place with good acoustics and we used Bälinge church. The acoustics there are really great and I played and played there for a week. Martin Igelström, the recording engineer, was fine to work with, and we were in agreement on the sound we were after.

In 1990 Olov Johansson became the first "World Champion of Nyckelharpa." The "Nyckelharpa World Cup" competition was established as a good-natured way of bringing the Swedish nyckelharpa community closer together and stirring up some folk music interest among the general public. It suggests, tongue in cheek, that as far as the nyckelharpa is concerned, Sweden is the "world." But the honor, good spirits and all, attests to Olov's musical skill and depth. I asked him about his background and beginnings, whether he had begun with classical training or something less formal.

I started to play different instruments on my own very early. My family had many different instruments — guitar, mandolin, organ, and more — and my mother played several of them. When I was eight I took piano lessons for about a year but that was so boring that I stopped. The only good aspect of that was that I learned how reading music works. I didn't learn to read but understood the scheme. The image I had from home of playing music was my mother and her sisters and brothers playing together at their family parties, jamming popular songs from when they were young, and dance tunes that my grandfather used to play. My piano lessons were something very different, and not nearly as appealing.

The first nyckelharpa I tried was my uncle's. Soon after that my mother bought one that I started to play. This was the first instrument I played that really captivated me. After playing on my own for a while I met Curt Tallroth, a famous nyckelharpa and fiddle player from Uppland province. He asked me to come and visit him and learn to play his tunes. Since then we play regularly together and we have a CD coming out this summer. So I guess I started with folk music even though I didn't know that was what it was when I started. I was just playing and having fun.

On Storsvarten *Olov plays both modern and older nyckelharpa, but also one cut on fiddle. I was surprised when I first saw the World Nyckelharpa Champion play fiddle, and wondered about this.*

I play the fiddle quite a lot, but not in Väsen. I play fiddle together with Curt Tallroth and with other fiddlers in Sweden, people like the well-known fiddlers Björn Ståbi and Mats Berglund. The fiddle is also a much more fun instrument to play when there are many people playing. You can hear yourself. At spelmansstämmor (fiddlers' gatherings) and parties I usually bring my fiddle. It's quick to tune and I can hear myself. The nyckelharpa is hard to keep in tune out of doors, and when there are many people playing, the instrument is too far from the ear to hear well.

It seems generally true that people who are really good at what they do expend the least effort doing it. Olov fits this pattern: he plays with little wasted motion, and his left-hand fingers always arrive in good time to where they're needed. He gives the impression of having put much thought and planning into his playing, of thoroughly understanding what he's doing and how he's approaching the music he's playing. I asked his thoughts about preparing to play a tune, what he does to work out his plan of attack.

I think for me this goes for nyckelharpa, fiddle and a lot of other activities in life. A tune is a whole consisting of details. Most music I play is dance music where it is the "groove" that is the base on which the tune is built. Everything in the tune must have its place and timing so it all comes together. When I learn a new tune I get a vision in my mind of how it should sound. I play and practice on the difficult parts until I am rather close to that vision. Then I further refine my mental image, and thus I have to practice more. I almost never come nearer than "rather close" when I play. This is what keeps me going.

Olov brings to his teaching the same well-thought-out clarity so evident in his playing. In a group class or one-on-one, he clearly presents and illustrates the concepts and the way they fit together. And he's gifted at listening to a student's playing and suggesting ways to improve, extend, grow. I was eager to hear the wisdom he might offer both students and teachers.

Teaching is interesting and difficult. No two students have the same needs. Some need help to hear what's going on in the music, some need help with physical technique and coordination. The teaching situation I like the most is like the one Curt [Tallroth] and I had. He was just there as a resource for me, and it was I who assigned myself my tasks while we were playing together. I listened, looked and asked. He gave me suggestions about tunes and so on, and if I liked them I learned them. It needs to be fun to learn and we had a really good time together.

As a student, you should decide what it is you want to learn, so you know what you are looking for from your teachers or when you're observing and studying good fiddlers. And when you practice, put your energy into the tunes, figures, passages you have a hard time playing. If it seems easy to practice, and it sounds good, then you're practicing the wrong stuff. Practice for the sake of practicing (and play for the sake of playing, too).

As we were running out of both time and publication space, I asked Olov if he had a tune to share, one that would work on fiddle as well as on nyckelharpa. He offered "Bisonpolska," a tune with links to both Sweden and the U.S.

I composed it in 1992, when I had returned from my first trip to the U.S., the "great country in the West." When we began to play it in Väsen, and the arrangement took form, we thought there was a flavor of America in it, and we collectively decided that "Bisonpolska" was an appropriate and amusing name. In Sweden "bison" is something foreign that we don't have, and "polska" is very common, so there's something self-contradicting in that name.

Väsen Discography

- *Väsen,* Drone (Sweden), 1990
- *Vilda Väsen,* Drone (Sweden), 1992
- *Essence,* Ethnic (France), 1993
- *Levande Väsen* (live in-concert recording), Drone (Sweden), 1996
- *Spirit* (compilation from first recordings, plus some new material), Northside, 1997

- *Whirled,* Northside, 1997
- *Storsvarten* (Olov solo), Northside, 1998

Northside, 530 N. 3rd St., Minneapolis, MN 55401; (612) 375-0233; http://www.noside.com
Drone: http://www.drone.se

[The American Nyckelharpa Association publishes an excellent newsletter covering technique, maintenance, and learning opportunities. For more information, write ANA, P.O. Box 2291, Chapel Hill NC 27515-2291.]

Bisonpolska

By Olov Johansson, from Väsen's *Spirit* album (Northside NSD6004) and *Vilda Väsen* (Drone). Transcription based on one by Elizabeth Weis.

A Matter of Tradition: A Conversation with Irish Fiddler James Kelly

By Hollis Payer

James Kelly is one of the most respected fiddlers playing traditional Irish music today. Through his many recordings, his involvement in such well known performing groups as Planxty and Patrick Street, and his teaching work in Irish music schools and festivals around the world, he has touched and inspired legions of musicians and music lovers. James' roots in the music run deep. He grew up in a musical household during a time of heightened interest in traditional music in Ireland. Like his father John before him, James is a font of information about tunes and anecdotes of characters who formed the tradition, and a fierce advocate of the music.

Tell me about the musical legacy you inherited from your father [John Kelly].

Well, I suppose to start at the very beginning — who said that, Julie Andrews? — my father was a musician, a fiddle player and a concertina player from a very rural part of County Clare, in the west of Ireland. He grew up where people didn't travel away very much, in fact they hardly ever traveled away. You had all your influences from the area you lived in, and the style of music that he played, of course, was a very traditional style. His concertina music, although he played the same dance tunes as he played on the fiddle, were settings for the concertina and he kept it separate, lovely ideas. He left County Clare in his late twenties and worked in the Bob of Allen, just outside Dublin. He met my mother and they got married in 1945 and set up a shop in Dublin, a little shop in Capel Street called The Horse Shoe. And they started a family. I was the youngest of five children and everybody was a musician in the house, including my mother who tipped a little bit on the accordion. Everybody else was a fiddle player in the family — six fiddlers. We had one piper, my brother Anthony who was also a fiddle player, but he was more a piper than a fiddler. We grew up together learning tunes, listening to tunes, old recordings, 78s, and tapes, and being visited by just an endless string of musicians, it seems.

How did it happen that there was this scene at your house? Was that from your father's old connections?

My father was one of the elder statesmen in the music, so to speak, a musician that people looked up to and revered. They respected his opinion very highly. He was an old-fashioned man — if you met him you'd think he was from the last century — he had this ancient feeling about him. He had a lot of knowledge about the music in him and if he responded to you favorably, you knew that you were doing something right within the tradition itself. Musicians loved to come to the house, they knew there'd always be a good welcome and they'd hear some music and talk. Through the years they made friends with a lot of people — he would travel a lot within Ireland itself, and he got to know a lot of people. People who didn't know him would come anyway....

Through your father and from your own experiences, you have particular insight into changes that have occurred in the culture and the traditional music of Ireland. What do you see from your perspective?

To go back a bit, before the 1930s, in Ireland people would get together in the rural parts of the country at the crossroads and the house dances and have their own social activities, dances, stories and songs. A family in the locality might have an old gramophone player, and when some of the 78 records would come from the States, it was like going to Disneyland! People would get together at whoever's house it would be and they'd listen to this record over and over and over again. It was a great time for excitement, you know. So that was going on when the early recordings were coming into Ireland from the States and the musicians who were making those recordings were becoming influential *because* they were making recordings... no one had made them before. Then in the '30s, there was a bit of a switch and the clergy in Ireland at the time played a role in that. They started to discourage the crossroad dances and the country dances and encourage people to go to the bigger towns and villages into these halls. In a sense it kind of put a stop to all that stuff, you know. The music itself went through a period in the '40s and '50s where there wasn't much going on at all. In a lot of cases people just played in their own homes — you might invite people in, get together and play. It wasn't as if you'd go for a festival like you would these days.

I was born in 1957. In Dublin in the late '50s, there were two plays going on. One of them was called *The Song of the Anvil,* and there were two groups of musicians together for those plays. One was a man called Sean O'Riada, and some of the other musicians were my father, Paddy Moloney, Michael Tubridy, Martin Fahey, Ronnie McShane, Sonny Brogan and Eamon DeBuitleir. Out of all that came the idea to form a group, which wasn't done before. Technically speaking, the idea of actually arranging folk music, or dance music, had been done on at least one or two 78 recordings that I have, but they were folk tunes done in a classical way, highly orchestrated. And I presume they

"I don't want to hear you copying my notes on a piece of paper. I want you to express yourself. I want you to be an individual, whether you're a singer or a dancer or a musician..."

were classical musicians. But in this case, they were all traditional musicians who called themselves Ceoltoiri Culainn. Ceoltoiri is the Gaelic word for musicians, and Culainn is a place name, just outside Dublin. The idea of the band was to present traditional songs with accompaniment and traditional dance tunes and slow airs, arranged with instruments: harpsichord, bodhran, piano, fiddle, flute, pipes, whistles. Sean O'Riada himself started to dig up the music of Turlough O'Carolan, and Ceoltoiri Culainn introduced the music of O'Carolan for the first time....In 1963, out of Ceoltoiri Culainn came the Chieftains, under the leadership of Paddy Moloney.

The kind of music that groups were playing was exposing people to a lot of different things in Ireland. Groups like Ceoltoiri Culainn were arranging music in a more basic way, with traditional instruments. People like Sweeney's Men were doing mainly blues stuff from the States, using an instrument never heard before in Ireland, the bouzouki. Ballad groups like the Clancy Brothers, the Dubliners, the Johnstons, the Pattersons were going strong in the '60s, traveling abroad a lot, influencing a lot of people. Country and western music was massive in the country, huge in Ireland in the '60s, cabaret acts as well. If you were an Irish musician, playing in Ireland in the '60s, the thought of you going into a pub locally to play a tune — I'm not talking about in a rural area, where that's the way they are, I'm talking about in the bigger places — they wouldn't let you in the door if they saw you coming with a fiddle or a flute.... When Capel Street was a pedestrian street, my father told me that when he walked down the street with his fiddle, they'd come out of the stores and jeer him, call him "Fiddler Kelly, Fiddler Kelly, Fiddler Kelly..." and when I was a kid they'd do the same thing to me. Well in the '70s, a lot of them weren't calling you Fiddler Kelly anymore. They saw you on TV, they heard you on the radio. And then it was, "Oh, I know *him.* Mr. Kelly, oh, I know Mr. Kelly, he has a shop up in Capel Street, he's a neighbor of mine." There was a fellow who used to sit on the back wall of the handball alley and jeer me. Then I didn't see him for a few years. I used to go to the Piper's Club up in Dublin at the time, up in Thomas Street...A few rooms, piano, sessions and all that going on. Well, I was standing there one night and the door opened and lo and behold who walked in, with a mandolin under his arm, to my astonishment, was my friend who used to jeer me all the time in the handball alley. And as he passed me by he says to me, "Hello, James." So times changed, you know. I was laughing when that happened.

You are constantly evolving as a musician, but you must have some sort of thought process guiding it toward your own notions of what traditional music is. Is that an intuitive sense, you know when you're going in the right direction and when you're not?

I think it has to do with the information that you've gathered and the exposure you've had over the years. When you've gathered a lot of information you have to sift through to figure out what you need. That's the wonderful thing about our brains, we can do it all in a second. You can make a decision when you play a dance tune, and improvise right on the spot and there's no thought. You're doing something different, you didn't think about doing it and you're doing it anyway. In my case, playing the dance tunes, who knows where I'm going to end up? When I play, my reference points are people like my father, Michael Coleman, Willie Clancy, Darach O'Cathain in singing, John McKenna playing the flute, Patsy Tuohy playing the pipes, and a lot of people that I haven't mentioned. That's where I'm coming from. See, they set all the standards for us. We're not waking up today in the '90s setting all these new standards. The standards have already been set....

Irish music is a music where you express yourself. It's not fixed. I don't give you a sheet and say, "Right, it's this way and that's the only way that you play them." What I say to you is this: "Here's a basic setting of this melody. Play it now and I want to hear *you* playing." I don't want to hear you copying my notes on a piece of paper. I want you to express yourself. I want you to be an individual, whether you're a singer or a dancer or a musician....

As a teacher, what do you recommend for someone trying to learn traditional Irish dance tunes?

...For me, at this particular stage it would be your knowledge of good basic technique. Now, people might think, "Oh, he wants us to be technicians of the instrument," and that's not what I mean. Basic knowledge and decent technique on your instrument — simple things like trying to keep your bow going somewhere between the middle of the bridge and the fingerboard. Bowing from your elbow as opposed to bowing from your shoulder. The angle of the instrument, and how you should be holding it under your jaw, against your body. Basic knowledge of the notes on your instrument, where they are, and how to do simple ornamentation. And not being too eager to learn many, many different dance tunes in a very short space of time. I would encourage people to take their time and give themselves a chance to put all those things into play that I just mentioned. You end up using a small amount of material, dance music, to help you practice. The repetition helps you to get better, and should include practice time dedicated to scales. Hand in hand with that of course is this appetite you need to develop to understand the music that you're trying to play, whatever it may be. I would encourage people to listen as much as possible. That's a big, big part of the equation right there, listening to the music.

...A lot of times if I'm coming upon new stuff that I haven't heard before, my tendency is not to go near it at all. I actually just listen, and let the tune sink in. Eventually I'll get down to trying to play it. As opposed to this terrible urge you see in people who are playing in sessions and they don't know the tune. An awful lot of them want to tip along with you. Not very many of them want to just sit back and listen and watch, be an observer. Now, what kind of participation is that? Wouldn't it be better if you just sat back and actually enjoyed listening to the piece? Enjoy listening to someone else play, and experience the visual aspect of learning. I like to pretend I'm the other person when learning stuff, trying to get a feel for it. For example, let's say your bow arm is not working really well, and you see another musician with a nice bow arm, it's good to visualize yourself with a nice bow arm! Imagine what it feels like to do the motion itself....

Technique is the answer. You have to dedicate yourself to learning that stuff. Anyone who does something that you admire, no matter what they do, all they've given you is an example of how they've developed and worked on their basic techniques. It's the same for all great artists.

I understand you've formed your own recording label now.

I'd been feeling like the music in certain ways has been suffering so I thought to hell with it, the only way I can make a statement about this stuff is that I can play the fiddle the way I play, and if I can, be involved with the production of records now and in the future. The label itself is called Capelhouse Records, and the first release is just *James Kelly*. In the past when I didn't have a name for tunes, I'd call them the Capelhouse this or that. Of course, the name itself is a story.

Discography

- *James Kelly* (with Paddy Keenan, Zan McLeod, Mark Stone and others), Capelhouse Records CD896012, 1997
- *Gaelic Roots* (Boston College Gaelic Roots Festival 1996), Kells KM-9514
- *Music in the Meadow* (Live from Wolf Trap, festival CD), Greater Washington Ceili Club
- *The Ring Sessions* (duet album with Zan McLeod), Claddagh Records
- *My Love Is In America* (with 16 Irish fiddlers in Boston, MA, 1990), Green Linnet 1110

- *Irish Times* (with Patrick Street), Green Linnet 1005
- *Capel Street* (solo album), Bowland Bow.0001
- *In Our Time* (with Danny McGinley), Bunnan Bui Bui-001B
- *Up The Airy Mountain* (with Sean O'Driscoll), Green Linnet 001
- *Sail Og Rua* (with Dolores Keane & John Faulkner), Gael-Linn
- *Words and Music* (with Planxty), Warner Bros. (WEA) 451
- *Spring In The Air* (with Paddy O'Brien & Daithi Sproule, Bowhand), Shanachie 29018

- *Is It Yourself* (with Paddy O'Brien & Daithy Sproule), Bowhand
- *Star of Munster* (with Ceoltoiri Leigheann), Gael-Linn CEF.047
- *Crooked Road* (with Ceoltoiri Leigheann), Gael-Linn, CEF.046
- *John & James Kelly* (fiddle duet), Tara 1008

[For bookings, or to order James' most recent CD, *James Kelly* ($15 + $2 s/h), or the cassette *Capel Street* ($10 + $2 s/h), contact Capelhouse Records, c/o Jay Hardy, 558 E. Bethel Rd., Bethel, ME 04217, (207) 875-2272.]

Lads of Laois

Traditional, arranged and transcribed by James Kelly, as played on his *James Kelly* CD (Capelhouse CD896012).
(Note: The following two tunes in the medley on the CD ("Gan Ainm" and "The Heathery Cruach") have not been transcribed.)

Limerick's Lamentation

Traditional, arranged by James Kelly. Transcribed by James Kelly and Jack Tuttle as played on James' *James Kelly* CD (Capelhouse CD896012).

This piece is played with a free time meter, thus the unusual notation. Since note durations are approximate,
the recording is essential to learn the feel of the tune. James Kelly plays this in the key of E on the recording by
tuning his fiddle low (E-B-F#-C#), but he fingers it in G major, as it is transcribed here. — Jack Tuttle

Barbara Lamb: Fiddler Fatale!

By Jack Tuttle

Whether it's bluegrass, western swing, Cajun fiddling or piecing together a string section, Barbara Lamb has shown great versatility that comes from her lifelong pursuit of various fiddle styles. Having spent the last several years with the popular Seattle-based band Ranch Romance, she recently has cut her reins and galloped off to the much less certain, sometimes precarious life of a freelance fiddler in the competitive Nashville music scene. This seemed like an opportune time to connect up and get some of her thoughts on Nashville, her career and the future.

You recently left the band Ranch Romance...

I just moved from my Northwest home of thirty-six years — which is all of my life — from there down here to Nashville. It's just so different, and so great. It's a huge move, not only geographically... but musically it's just completely different. There are so many good acoustic players — electric as well, but acoustic being the world that I live in. It's very challenging and wonderfully inspiring, and mind boggling how many good fiddle players there are here. It's really pretty terrific.

So what kinds of things are you doing now there?

I've become a free-lance fiddle player, as opposed to being a band member, and I've always been a band member up until just recently, leaving Ranch Romance. So I am doing everything from playing the kind of cliché hookline of Beethoven's 9th solo violin in Carnegie Hall, to playing strum-up, strum-up, strum-up back-up guitar as a multi-instrumentalist sideman in Nashville. And everything in between...They tend to be commercial jingles, fiddle lines, violin lines that range from ten seconds to thirty seconds...A real variety of stuff. You pretty much have to be ready for anything that gets thrown your way. I haven't played the tuba yet. I think I will.

Do a lot of the fiddle players there have a classical background, or are you unusual in that?

I think a lot of fiddle players do have classical backgrounds. It's funny — the classical question comes up quite often. I think the way I play suggests technique-wise that I've been a classical player. I've never been a classical player. I did take violin lessons when I was a kid. I never dug it — as a matter of fact, I cried often. They were so boring, my violin lessons. But I took classical technique lessons from the time I was eight until I was eleven. Somehow or another in there I managed to learn a thing or two, like how to hold the instrument properly so it would be easy to play, how to do vibrato, how to shift positions — those pretty big things that come in oh-so-handy, with whatever style you're playing... But now people say, "You've played classical violin, haven't you?" And at first I really was offended by that somehow — I felt that maybe my playing was stiff or staid somehow, but now I take that as a compliment — that there's good technique there. I think that most violin players, fiddle players — especially in Nashville — professionals, have classical backgrounds. It sure helps. I taught for a hundred million years — actually I taught for probably fourteen years — and I felt like I was teaching my students a classical technique using fiddle tunes as the exercises.

So at age eleven, when you quit taking violin lessons, did you switch right to fiddling?

I did, but not American fiddling. My parents were really involved in the Scandinavian dance community in Seattle, and I would tag along with them to the dances, and they had live fiddlers. And it was such cool music. They didn't have guitars or accordions. Every once in a while somebody might play another instrument, but it was mostly fiddlers, and it was any number from one to fifty fiddlers. And the music is very beautiful...This fiddler named "Fiddling John" kind of took me under his wing. He was in his fifties, and here I was eleven, and he taught me some tunes. I could read music, and all of this stuff was written down, so I started learning those tunes and going to the dances, and playing along with that big throng of fiddle players. I did that for about a year, and then I became a regular fiddle player at the dances that my parents were in. At one point, we were all doing a show together — the dance group was doing a show, the fiddle players were doing their part of the show, it was a real variety of things, and there was this bluegrass band there. The fiddle player was a woman named Vivian Williams. I flipped. She played the "Orange Blossom Special," and here I was, twelve, and it was right then that I knew that was how it was going to be. I begged my father to ask Vivian to give me fiddle lessons, and she did. And I took lessons from her probably till I was about fourteen, fifteen, and it really became my social life. Vivian and I released an album on Voyager Records

Photo: Benham Studios

"...People say, 'You've played classical violin, haven't you?' And at first I really was offended by that somehow — I felt that maybe my playing was stiff or staid somehow, but now I take that as a compliment — that there's good technique there."

called *Twin Sisters* — it's now almost twenty years ago that that came out. So classical, to Swedish music, to bluegrass. But a lot of old-time. I learned all the fiddle tunes I could learn and entered all the contests I could enter, then started playing with bluegrass bands. From bluegrass bands, people got very experimental; we started playing some Bob Wills tunes. By the time I was eighteen, I think, I started playing in a country band.

Let's talk a little about your playing and keeping your chops up.

...When I moved — and this is one of the reasons I moved out of Seattle to Nashville, to get a whole new perspective on things — at first I didn't have any kind of playing situations that I was in except in my living room. So I started practicing two and three hours a day again, which I haven't done since I was maybe fourteen or fifteen years old. Played all kinds of fiddle tunes, all kinds of bluegrass tunes. It's true what they say — if you practice (as much as I hate it!) — if you practice a lot, your chop gets back together... So right now I feel like my skills are up there, which is one of the thrilling things about being a freelance player. You play jazz one day, you play bluegrass another day, you play guitar another day — you're getting all this different input all the time. For me, it works. It makes me a better player. I still hate to practice! Maybe if you don't call it practicing—what could we call it? I don't know, because I also hate to rehearse.

Does your practicing mostly consist of playing? If you want to get your bluegrass chops up for instance, do you just play bluegrass, or do you do special exercises?

I'll play a tune. Right now I'm preparing material for the next fiddle album, so I play things from start to finish. I don't really work on a difficult fingering thing or a position change. What I do for myself is the same thing I do for teaching. If I'm having difficulty with something technically, I will get a tune or even make up a tune that has that in it as an exercise. I bore so easily that I like playing melodies. So if you're playing a melody and it's got some tricky fingering in it, it's just a cleverly disguised exercise.

Do you have any advice for aspiring fiddlers?

I wish I had some sort of new advice. It's sort of like losing weight: Don't eat so much. To get good, you've got to play a lot and practice a lot. I think that my main advice would be to play the kind of music that you like. It didn't start happening for me until I started playing the music that I liked, which, at the time, was Scandinavian dance music. I think sometimes players make a mistake in that they feel they've got to put in some time, so many years or whatever, of grueling scales and études and various violin exercises before they can really start having fun. Now, I think all of that is extremely valuable, if you like it, but above all else, if you're not having fun, you're not going to practice, you're not going to "do" the instrument. So find a teacher that will teach you things that are fun to play, along with the technique at the same time. But then, I'm just that kind of person. I won't do anything unless it's got a certain amount of fun to it.

[Since 1997, Barbara has been involved with a new fiddle camp, The Nashville Acoustic Music and Songwriting Camp (NashCamp for short), held outside Nashville each June. NashCamp offers two sessions of instruction: a bluegrass session and a songwriting session. During the bluegrass session, in addition to fiddle with Barbara Lamb and Fletcher Bright, classes are offered in Dobro, bass, guitar, and mandolin. For more information: www.nashcamp.com; NashCamp@aol.com; P.O. Box 90031, Nashville, TN 37209; 888-798-5012.]

Discography

- *Shum Ticky,* with The Laura Love Band, 1999, Mercury
- *Tonight I Feel Like Texas,* 1997, Sugar Hill
- *Fiddle Fatale,* 1993, Sugar Hill SH-3810
- *Flip City,* with Ranch Romance, 1993, Sugar Hill SH-3813

- *Blue Blazes,* with Ranch Romance, 1991, Sugar Hill SH-3794
- *Western Dream,* with Ranch Romance, 1989, 1992, Sugar Hill SH-3799
- *Twin Sisters,* with Vivian Williams and Tall Timber, 1975, Voyager Recordings VRLP 316-S

Sugar Hill Records, (800) 996-4455
Voyager Recordings, (206) 323-1112

For bookings, contact Barbara at BabsLamb@aol.com

Road to Silverton

By Barbara Lamb and Laura Love (Barbara Lamb, Let 'er Buck Music (ASCAP), ©1998). Transcribed by Jack Tuttle.

Laurie Lewis on Fiddling

By Mary Larsen

Singer, songwriter, and fiddler extraordinaire, Laurie Lewis is one talented performer. Raised in Berkeley, California, she was first introduced to bluegrass and old-time music during the folk boom of the '60s. In the early '70s, she began playing and singing bluegrass as the bassist in San Francisco's Phantoms of the Opry with Pat Enright. Laurie has toured and performed with artists as diverse as Sam Bush, Holly Near, Peter Rowan, the Good Ol' Persons, Blue Rose, and her own band, Grant Street. She has received numerous awards from the International Bluegrass Music Association, the National Association of Independent Record Distributors, among others, and has appeared on PBS' "Lonesome Pine Specials," TNN's "The Texas Connection," and "The Grand Ole Opry." Her current project, "Laurie Lewis and Her Bluegrass Pals," is a return to the classic bluegrass band format, with Tom Rozum, Todd Phillips, Craig Smith, and Mary Gibbons (on mandolin, bass, banjo and guitar, respectively). I asked Laurie about her fiddle playing, from her classical violin lessons as a teenager to her show-stopping bluegrass breaks now.

Photo: Anne Hamersky

Did you start with classical lessons?

Yeah, I did. I started playing classical violin when I was twelve years old. I didn't choose the violin. It was understood that music lessons were a part of education in my family. My parents thought that I had a good ear and that the violin would be a good choice. Being the dutiful daughter, I said "okay."

How did you get into bluegrass?

It was years later. I had quit playing violin... I hated violin. [Laughter] Well, I didn't enjoy my lessons. I loved the instrument and I hated taking lessons. I had a lot of personal angst involved with the violin, so when I could, I quit. As soon as I graduated high school and left home, I stopped playing the violin. It lived under my bed. I didn't get into bluegrass music until years later — I was twenty-two, twenty-three years old. My older sister asked me to do music at her wedding — a very small, family get-together. When I was fourteen, I began playing guitar and singing folk songs and became quite enamored of the music of Doc Watson and the popular folk heroes of the day: Dylan, Baez, the Dillards, etc. So I guess my sister had something like that in mind. I said sure, and then somehow got the idea that I would learn some fiddle waltzes off of an old Chubby Wise record that I had had for years. It's funny: I played the violin, had listened to and loved these tunes for years, but until my sister's wedding, it had never occurred to me that I could play them. And that was it — I was completely taken with the fiddle.

How and how often do you practice?

Practicing is difficult now because of time constraints. I have very little time when I'm just relaxed and can pick up the fiddle without the phone ringing or something else happening, calling my attention away, and just really applying myself to practice. The kind of practice that helps me the most is learning solos note-for-note, really trying to get into another fiddler's head. This makes my fingers move in patterns that I wouldn't think of on my own. It really stretches my horizons and is great ear training.

One approach that I have to teaching is to take, say, a Benny Martin solo from a classic Flatt and Scruggs recording, and learn it and teach it simultaneously to the class. Often it means slowing the tape down to half-speed and really laboring over some minute detail, but the rewards are powerful, and it teaches the students how to learn on their own. I'm speaking of the week-long intensive classes that I teach at Bluegrass at the Beach in Nehalem Bay, Oregon.

How much of what you do on stage is improvisation, and how much is worked out?

I would say most of it starts out being improvisation, but for me, after I've played the song a number of times I get pretty much set in a way of doing it and it tends to not stray too far from that way of playing it. If it's a fiddle tune I improvise less on it than a break to a song or something like that. I would say that also has to do with the different directions in which I'm pulled in the band. If you're doing MC

"We as a society get very divorced from...the idea that you can actually pick up a guitar, a fiddle, whatever, and play. There are the musicians, and there are the other people. The other people think, 'How do they do that?' They're probably all musicians too. They just don't know it."

work, and then you're singing a song, and then you play a fiddle break, and then you go into the next verse...my mind just doesn't think that fast, it can't get a brand new idea going really fast. But somebody like Stuart Duncan is amazing that way. He always plays differently, and he's kind of a consummate bluegrass fiddler in that way — very improvisational, and always taking off in new directions.

Do you have any tips or advice for beginners?

I think it can be very helpful to read music, but it also really helps to follow your ear. After all, you can only play what you can hear. Playing with regularity is very important — on the fiddle perhaps more than many other instruments. Since it doesn't have frets, you really have to train your hands. You can't just be a weekend warrior on the fiddle and expect to progress. You've got to play a little bit every day. Here I am telling you advice that I should follow, but I think that if you can even manage fifteen minutes a day of concentrated practice, not just doodling on the fiddle, but real concentrated practice, that would be better than doing an hour every four days. It's also easier on you physically. The fiddle can be a most uncomfortable instrument to play. There is often a lot of back and neck tension involved, so remembering to stay limber and relaxed is very important.

Do you have any ideas about how to get more young people involved in traditional music?

It's tough because, as you know, this is music that you have to seek out. You're not going to find much of it at all on any kind of mainstream venue. It's not on MTV, that's for sure. It's hard for young people to even know that it exists. There's such a joy in the community that happens so much in bluegrass and old-time music circles, a coming together and sharing of tunes and the actual hands-on playing of music. It's a difficult question. With the advent of mass media, the passing on of family traditions and the idea of music as recreation has fallen by the wayside. It's something that people always worry about: "Where's the future of the music? How are young people going to find out about this?" But things that really help are great young players like Alison Krauss, out there getting a lot more mainstream acceptance, just standing up there and playing the fire out of the fiddle. She's probably done a lot to draw younger people to the music, as has Jerry Garcia. If *he* plays the banjo, it must be cool!

I was at the International Bluegrass Music Association Awards show recently, and as part of the show they had a bluegrass band of twelve and thirteen year olds, and they were fantastic. They had been put together from all over the country, which I thought was really neat. But in a way it's sad, because you can't get a group of kids from any one area very easily that are so proficient as these kids were. The fact that they could come from all over the country and really play together and sound like a band almost immediately was really something. They had a couple of hours of rehearsal time together, then they got up and played, and they were great.

I think it would be very helpful to have more music programs in schools, but of course that's like a pipe dream these days because everything's getting cut to the bone, and of course, music gets cut before everything else. I know it was really important to me growing up to have the music in the schools. It's just a shame that there's not more of it. We (my band and I) sometimes go out and play school shows and workshops for kids. I wish that there were some kind of funding to make that a more viable thing for us to do, because I think it's so important. Exposure is the main thing. If younger people hear the music, they have a chance of deciding whether they like it, and they have the chance of being involved in the making of music. We as a society get very divorced from that — the idea that you can actually pick up a guitar, a fiddle, whatever, and play. There are the musicians, and there are the other people. The other people think, "How do they do that?" They're probably all musicians too. They just don't know it. It's probably better for us working musicians, though — let's keep it an exclusive club!

Discography

- *Laurie Lewis and Her Bluegrass Pals,* 1999 (Rounder 0461)
- *Seeing Things,* 1998 (Rounder 0428)
- *Earth and Sky: Songs of Laurie Lewis,* 1997 (Rounder 0400)
- *True Life Blues: The Songs of Bill Monroe,* Various Artists, 1996 (Sugar Hill 2209)
- *The Oak and the Laurel,* with Tom Rozum, 1995 (Rounder 0340)
- *True Stories,* 1993 (Rounder 0300)
- *Together,* with Kathy Kallick, 1995 (Rounder 0318; orig. Kaleidoscope, 1991)
- *Singing My Troubles Away,* with Grant Street, 1990 (Flying Fish 515)
- *Love Chooses You,* 1989 (Flying Fish 487)
- *Blue Rose,* Blue Rose, 1988 (Sugar Hill 3768)
- *Restless Rambling Heart,* 1986 (Flying Fish 406)

Rounder Records, (800) 44-DISCS; http://www.rounder.com

For information on recordings, tours, etc., see Laurie's website at http://www.laurielewis.com, or contact her at Spruce and Maple Music, P.O. Box 9417, Berkeley, CA 94709-0417; email: laurie@laurielewis.com

For information on bookings, contact Cash Edwards at Under the Hat Productions, 1121-B Bluebonnet Lane, Austin, TX 78704, (512) 447-0544; email: uthp@earthlink.net

Big Eddy

By Laurie Lewis and Tom Rozum, Spruce and Maple Music (ASCAP). Transcribed by Jack Tuttle as
played by Laurie Lewis on her album *Laurie Lewis and Her Bluegrass Pals* (Rounder 0461)

*"Tom and I made up this tune on a three-day rafting trip down the lovely Rio Chama in northern New Mexico. Just below
the place we disembarked is the official Big Eddy, but this tune is about the smaller big eddy further upstream. By not resolving
the B part until after the long tag, we tried to emulate the way an eddy turns back against the general current, and makes
at least a small section of river run upstream. Of course, it eventually spits you back into the current again."* — Laurie Lewis

Sandy MacIntyre: "Born to Fiddle"

By Henry McGuirk

Photo: Claire McGuirk

Sandy has been composing, playing, teaching and promoting the Cape Breton style of Celtic music for some forty years. He spent five years with the CBC national television program *Ceilidh,* and spent several years touring and recording with the Cape Breton Symphony. Today, Sandy appears at special shows, concerts and workshops in Canada and abroad, including tours to Scotland, the Northwest Territories, and California. He was a feature artist in the hit Celtic musical production "Needfire" during the summer of 1998, plays regularly at select clubs around Ontario, and performs annually at the Canadian National Exhibition and at Harbour Centre in Toronto. Sandy teaches traditional fiddle and stepdancing four times weekly, with private students and in group classes, and received the "Best Music Teacher in Toronto" award as voted on by the readers of *NOW Magazine.* He has spent every summer for the past twelve years directing the Cape Breton fiddle program at St. Anne's Gaelic College in Cape Breton.

Sandy MacIntyre was immersed in music from day one. His grandfather, mother, and brothers and sisters all played fiddle, piano or guitar. Some were stepdancers. "I was born and bred in music…Our home in Inverness, Nova Scotia, on a Sunday afternoon was a gathering place for Cape Breton fiddlers, pipers, dancers and gaelic singers." Sandy was especially influenced by Winston "Scotty" Fitzgerald, Angus Chisolm, Dan J. Campbell and Angus Alan Gillis. "They played the old style of Cape Breton fiddling with the old style of bowing which is the same as my mother and grandfather played. Those fiddlers of a bygone era are the ones that raised the bar that we all strive to reach today. I played by ear the first couple of years and then started to read music. Actually, I never had a music scale ever shown to me or a music lesson, so I picked up everything on my own, as did most Cape Breton fiddlers at the time." *(Text continued on page 70.)*

The Sound of Mull

Traditional. Transcribed by Jack Tuttle as played by Sandy MacIntyre on his *Island Treasure, Vol. 1* recording.

Major Molle's Reel

Traditional. Transcribed by Jack Tuttle as played by Sandy MacIntyre on his *Island Treasure, Vol. 1* recording.

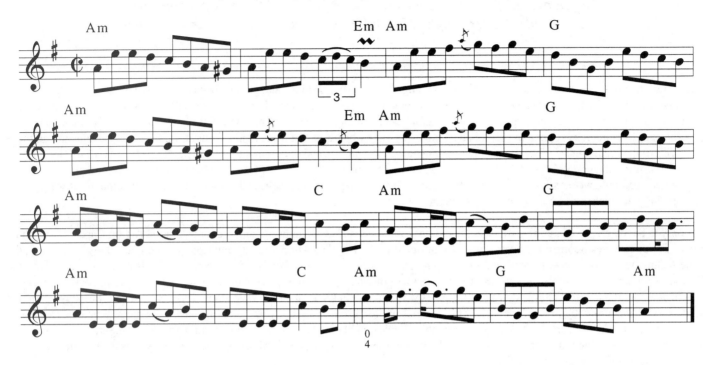

Miss C. Crawford's Reel

By Robert Mackintosh. Transcribed by Jack Tuttle as played by Sandy MacIntyre on his *Island Treasure, Vol. 1* recording.

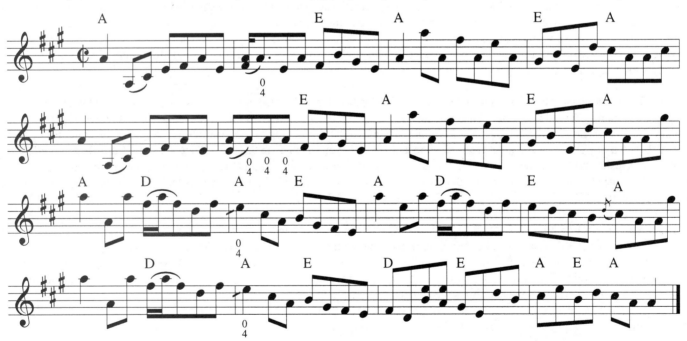

Note: To play these three tunes along with the CD, remove the last note (A) from the first two pieces and play each tune twice.
— *Jack Tuttle*

*"When playing for a square dance, a Cape Breton fiddler may play upwards
of two hundred tunes a night. Most fiddlers literally know thousands of tunes."*

Sandy started playing the fiddle at about age sixteen, having started earlier on piano and guitar, "because everyone else played the fiddle." When he was eighteen, he left Inverness for Toronto. "I could play a very few tunes. I knew thousands of tunes in my head just dying to come out somewhere… I was living in a third floor flat in Toronto, all alone in one room, and missing the music terribly. I decided I was going to start learning how to read music. I had a lot of time on my hands at that time, that's about all I had — lots of time and all these memories of the great music." Sandy was soon running dances in Toronto, and once a month invited his fiddle heroes from Cape Breton, such as Winston Fitzgerald, Angus Chisholm, Donald Angus Beaton, and Buddy MacMaster. "We would fly them in to Toronto, where they would spend the weekend. I spent a lot of time with Winston Fitzgerald and Angus Chisholm when they'd come in. It was a lot of fun, playing with them and learning things from them."

Not only is Sandy a fervent traditionalist and tireless performer, he is also a sought-out and recognized authority on Cape Breton fiddle music. Sandy believes Scottish music was born and nurtured in the Highlands of Scotland centuries ago and that same music, using the same techniques, is what was later played in the Highlands of Cape Breton. When the Scots were driven from their land during the Clearances, many of them settled in Cape Breton and various other places throughout the United States and Canada. There was a break in the music in Scotland at that time; fiddles and bagpipes were banned in the Highlands. When they did eventually start to play again and tried to revive the music, there was a classical influence to it and so the old Scottish style of fiddling was lost to them. When the Highlands immigrants first came to Cape Breton, they brought their fiddles and bagpipes with them and continued to play the traditional style, so there was no break in the music and the Scottish style of centuries ago can still be heard in Cape Breton today. It is the real thing, handed down from generation to generation.

"When we play Cape Breton fiddle, we automatically think 'dancing.' When playing strathspeys, for instance, we pay attention to the dotted notes and round them out in a more even and flowing rhythm, unlike present day Scottish fiddlers, who play a much more strict, pronounced and rigid tempo. Cape Breton fiddlers play slow airs, marches, clogs, hornpipes, strathspeys, jigs and reels. Cape Breton fiddling offers a tremendous driving force which usually brings dancers to their feet and instant toe-tapping from seasoned listeners and those hearing our music for the first time. We keep a rhythmic beat to our music by tapping our feet — sometimes one foot, other times both feet using different beats depending on the tempo. For example, when tapping to reels, we normally use a rocking motion of the foot between the heel and toe. We usually tap the heel in keeping time to the jig, march and strathspey. Most Cape Breton fiddlers, especially dance players, play with great energy and spirit and with a lot of 'drive' at a medium speed. Playing 'lively' is not to be confused with playing fast. When playing for a square dance, a Cape Breton fiddler may play upwards of two hundred tunes a night. Most fiddlers literally know thousands of tunes."

Sandy offers this advice for fiddlers interested in learning the Cape Breton style: "Get involved as soon as possible. Don't get too tied up with the note reading. Try to single out an older fiddler, or a younger one, who has a lot of the old style bowing. Fiddlers like John Morris Rankin, Natalie MacMaster, and Ashley MacIsaac play the old style. Try to single someone out, or, very simply, come to the Gaelic College! And try to get into a couple of sessions, sit in and see what you can pick up that way. There are some Cape Breton fiddlers who do not read music, and I hope they never start, because they're just great players. Sometimes reading music will ruin a person's style. I would say to listen to a lot of tapes of the old style of Cape Breton fiddling and attend Cape Breton fiddle workshops in your area whenever possible."

Sandy MacIntyre will continue his active pace of performances, workshops and classes as he travels wherever the music takes him. During the summer of 1999, Sandy will be performing and conducting workshops at the California Traditional Music Society Summer Solstice Festival, and at the Festival of American Fiddle Tunes in Port Townsend, Washington. Sandy will also be appearing at the 1999 Celtic Colours Festival in Cape Breton in October. Cape Breton fiddle music has been a big part of his life and now he is having the time of his life. To Sandy, fiddling is *fun* and should be enjoyed to the fullest.

Discography

- *Steeped in Tradition* (Sandy MacIntyre Productions Inc. SMCD 9607)
- *Island Treasure, Vol. 1* (Sandy MacIntyre Productions Inc. SM 9107)
- *Let's Have a Ceilidh* (Sandy MacIntyre Productions Inc. CLP 1001C)
- *Cape Breton, My Land In Music* (Sandy MacIntyre Productions Inc. SMC 1002C)

- Video: *Carrying on the Traditions: Cape Breton Scottish Fiddling Today* (Fiddler Magazine)

[For information on recordings, bookings, lessons and workshops, contact: Sandy MacIntyre, 1 Aberfoyle Crescent, Suite 1702, Etobicoke, Ontario, M8X 2X8, Canada; (416) 231-8717.]

[The Gaelic College of Celtic Arts and Crafts, which offers sessions in July and August, can be contacted at P.O. Box 9, Baddeck, N.S., Canada B0E 1B0, (902) 295-3411.]

Cape Breton's Natalie MacMaster: Taking on the World

By Mary Larsen

Cape Breton's Natalie MacMaster has taken her fiddling and dance talent all over the world, and has played with musicians as varied as Joan Osborne, The Chieftains, Martin Hayes, and Carlos Santana. She has won a host of awards, most recently the 1999 East Coast Music Awards' "Female Artist of the Year" and a JUNO ("Best Instrumental Album of the Year") for her 1998 album *My Roots Are Showing*. Always a crowd pleaser, Natalie's fiddle and step dance finale was called "the best seven minutes in show business" by a Nashville producer.

After a number of traditional albums, Natalie showed her interest in a wide range of styles with her 1997 *No Boundaries* album. Her latest, *My Roots Are Showing*, brings her back to her traditional Cape Breton roots. Always eager for new challenges, Natalie's next album will once again diverge from the traditional and explore more contemporary musical styles.

Natalie started step dancing at age five, under the instruction of her mother Minnie. She began fiddling at

Photo: KOCH

age nine, learning first from her father and a bit later from Stan Chapman, a teacher in Antigonish, on the northeast mainland of Nova Scotia. Within six months of first picking up a fiddle, Natalie played at her first concert. She began playing for dances at age twelve, and shortly thereafter, she began traveling, playing in Boston at thirteen, Vancouver at fourteen, and now having performed almost everywhere from London to Tokyo, it would probably be easier to list the places she hasn't played!

Natalie credits her uncle Buddy MacMaster as being the greatest influence on her fiddling, as his recordings were constantly heard in her home, growing up. Other influences, and recordings often heard around the house, include Angus Chisholm, Donald Angus Beaton, Winston "Scotty" Fitzgerald, Cameron Chisholm, Arthur Muise, Jerry Holland, and Willie Kennedy. More recently, she has been influenced by Irish-American fiddler Eileen Ivers, and also has a few Mark O'Connor tunes in her repertoire. Natalie says, "It's mostly the tunes that attract me as far as my playing other types of music. I never really learned a particular style, other than Cape Breton, but I've played a lot of Irish tunes, and I just play them my own way. I play a few Texas swing tunes, because I like them, and I don't really play them Texas swing style — I play them in my own style. I haven't really concentrated on any other styles, but I certainly enjoy listening to them."

Natalie learns most of her tunes from tapes, but also learns "the odd tune from people, especially Dave MacIsaac — he plays with me a lot and he's always jigging [singing] tunes. I get them off his mouth, really — he jigs them and I learn them. Also a few by note —when I'm really, really hungry for new tunes, I'll pull out a book…"

Asked to single out an especially memorable musical experience, Natalie said: "One of my most exciting musical experiences was at the Mark O'Connor fiddle camp in October 1995. Mark O'Connor and Darol Anger and Ian Swensen were all playing — actually Mark was in the lead — they were all down sitting on the wharf on the lake, and it was about two or three in the morning. All you could hear was three fiddles in harmony, playing. Mark was playing stuff he had never played before, just improvising, doing everything you can imagine, and the other two guys backing him up. You could just hear them and the crickets. It was a full moon, and every now and again you'd hear a fish pop out of the water. It was amazing — definitely one of my highlights."

Natalie offers the following advice for young fiddlers interested in fiddling, and especially the Cape Breton style: "Stick with it. It's very rewarding, and it's always the times that I didn't want to — not that I ever practiced a whole lot anyway — but the times that I just didn't feel like practicing, if I pushed myself that little bit extra, it did me a world of good. A person should keep that in mind when they're trying to learn something, just to stick with it for the extra — even if it's just ten minutes, until you get what it is you're trying to do. It will definitely pay off for you in the long run."

Being on tour so much, Natalie says she doesn't have time to practice as much as she'd like. "I've been playing every day, I've been warming up before each show — I usually play for a half an hour, and that involves a bit of practicing, I guess, but as far as real practice,

"The times that I just didn't feel like practicing, if I pushed myself that little bit extra, it did me a world of good. A person should keep that in mind when they're trying to learn something, just to stick with it for the extra — even if it's just ten minutes, until you get what it is you're trying to do."

or what I think is practice, which is picking out your mistakes, and trying to make it better, I haven't done that in quite a while. And I need to — I'm not saying I don't. But I haven't had the time. When you're playing music every day, you don't want to take your free time, whatever there is, and sit there and really practice. But don't tell that to the ones who are learning, because I just told them to take the extra ten minutes!"

I asked Natalie if she ever gets tired of being on the road so much. "Oh, yeah, I do. I'm on the road all the time. I haven't had a vacation, really, ever. So that part gets tiring. But I just try not to think about the future, like when I think about what I'm doing two weeks ahead, or a month ahead, I'll be like, 'Oh, no, I have no rest, no break!' But I try not to think like that. I just take it one day at a time, and usually every day is good, there's something — a really nice thing we were playing at, or I meet somebody new, or I learn a new tune or something."

Discography

Feature Albums:
* *In My Hands* (1999)
* *My Roots Are Showing* (1998)
* *No Boundaries* (1997)
* *Fit As A Fiddle* (1993)
* *Road to the Isle* (1991)
* *Four on the Floor* (1989)
* *A Compilation* (CD release of *Road to the Isle* and *Four on the Floor*)

Instructional Video:
* *A Fiddle Lesson* (1997)

Rounder Records, One Camp Street, Cambridge, MA 02140, (800) 44-DISCS; http://www.rounder.com
Warner Music Canada, Ltd., 3751 Victoria Park Ave., Scarborough, Ontario, Canada M1W 3Z4; (416) 491-5005; Fax: (416) 491-8203.

For information on Natalie, her tour schedule, or her recordings, see her website at http://www.macmastermusic.com, or write MacMaster Music Inc., R.R. 1, Port Hastings, Nova Scotia, Canada B0E 2T0
Email: natalie@ns.sympatico.ca

For bookings, contact André Bourgeois at (902) 632-2575; Fax: (902) 632-2576.

The Lass of Carrie Mills

Traditional strathspey. Transcribed by Jack Tuttle as played by Natalie MacMaster
on her *Fit As A Fiddle* album (Rounder CD 7022/Warner Music Canada)

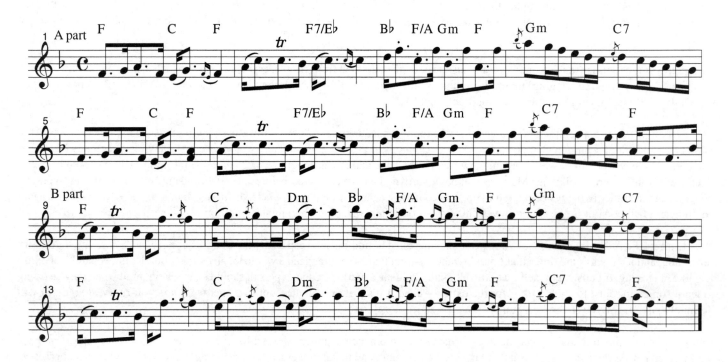

Frankie McWhorter:
Cowboy and Ranch Dance Fiddler

By Lanny Fiel

Photo: Mike Calcote

The name of Frankie McWhorter is likely to come up early when the topic of conversation turns to Texas fiddlers. Having worked with western swing legends such as the Miller Brothers (1957-1959) and Bob Wills (1960-1962), he has earned a place among the top players from the Lone Star State. Nowadays, he often appears with former members of the Texas Playboys and fronts his own band for dances around the Texas Panhandle. None of these activities is unusual for a professional musician of this caliber, unless you take into account that this wiry, silver-haired gentleman primarily makes his living as a working cowboy. From that standpoint, the name of Frankie McWhorter takes on a whole new dimension.

As a youngster, Frankie grew up in a country home in Hall County, Texas, singing at his mother's side and playing French harmonica just as she did. His uncle, Floyd Tucker, won the Alabama fiddle championship several times, but the instrument did not initially take hold with Frankie. His early years were spent singing and listening to his grandfather I.J. Tucker play the pump organ. "Pa" Tucker was a prominent composer who penned but sold his rights to "Wait for the Wagon," "Be My Life's Companion and You'll Never Grow Old," and "Let a Smile Be Your Umbrella on a Rainy Day." "Most of the time we just sang and played for each other," Frankie remembers. "We had a radio, but we only played it for the news to keep from running down the batteries."

Having grown up with music as a part of everyday life, Frankie continued the tradition wherever he went. Still in his teens, he began breaking horses after school for legendary horse trainer Boyd Rogers. Rogers also played fiddle and took note of the young ranch hand's natural inclination for music while on a trip to New York. The two had set out in a 1923 Dodge truck to deliver a load of polo ponies they had trained. With no passenger seat, Frankie rode atop a five-gallon bucket using a saddle blanket for a cushion while whistling, singing, and playing harmonica. The elder Rogers supplied requests and encouragement. "You ought to be playing fiddle," Rogers suggested. "You can already whistle anything you want." Frankie took the advice to heart, learning tunes from Rogers whenever he could. Often his new mentor encouraged fiddling to cool tempers whenever an ornery horse proved difficult.

During these times, the Wills standard "Faded Love" had reached the top of the charts, and Frankie poured dimes into a café jukebox until he knew it by heart. Upon demonstrating his accomplishment to Rogers, the elder fiddler commented, "You're playing that tune too slow, son. Where did you hear that?" Rogers knew the melody as "Forsaken Lover," an earlier, more up-tempo version as it had been played at an old "Trapper Rendezvous."

Frankie continued to broaden his repertoire as he drifted more in the direction of cowboy and ranch work. Protesting an overzealous inclination to "give one too many whippings," he left school and signed on as a cowhand for the JA Ranch founded by Texas legend, Charlie Goodnight. There, in addition to working cattle, Frankie began learning breakdowns from wagon boss Bud Long, who whistled tunes around the chuck wagon while Frankie tried his hand on the fiddle.

Eventually, Rogers arranged to have renowned Texas fiddler Eck Robertson travel on weekends from Amarillo to ranch country to teach the young fiddler. Frankie learned tunes and techniques such as keeping time with the bow in case a guitarist failed to show for a dance. Robertson's style represented an era when cowfolk held dances in country homes cleared of furniture to make way for dancing. At such times, a lone fiddler often stood in a doorway, playing for dancers in adjoining rooms.

Of his childhood, Frankie recalls one of these ranch dances when Bob Wills was the lone fiddler. Unfortunately, Frankie as a boy only caught a fleeting glimpse of Wills before a matronly attendant shooed him to a back bedroom with the other small children. Little did he know at the time that he would eventually tour and perform with this Texas legend. Frankie now holds the distinction of being the 463rd member of Bob Wills and His Texas Playboys.

"You have the same 'feel' for the fiddle as Bob Wills," Boyd Rogers once told Frankie. Recognizing the uncanny resemblance to Wills in Frankie's fiddling, Rogers referred to that raw, frontier fiddle sound rooted in West Texas cow camps, cotton fields, and vast plains. Wills had been raised playing for country and ranch dances in this setting and had built a legacy on the fiddle tradition of his father John Wills and maternal uncle, Tom Foley. In comparing Frankie's touch to the Wills family sound, Rogers heard an intangible quality that speaks of this same experience of life in the West.

"Likely as not, especially if guests arrive, [Frankie] will be up late into the night playing like there was no tomorrow but still be ready early the next morning for a day's work."

During his years touring with Wills, Frankie kept this tradition in mind. Amidst the glitz and glamour of Las Vegas, the newcomer in the fiddle section often persuaded the "Old Man" to take a moment backstage and teach him the old tunes played by papa John Wills. Wills thought no one would be interested in "those old things." But with a passion, Frankie committed Wills' recollections to memory and continues today to perform them unchanged. The same holds true for the tunes he learned from Eck Robertson and Boyd Rogers.

More often than not, these old tunes can now be heard coming from the foreman's house on the Malouf Abraham Ranch where Frankie manages seventeen sections of prime Texas ranchland. During the day, he may break momentarily from tending livestock to take up a fiddle, recalling a melody or harmony part that comes to mind — a throwback to his days of working with Boyd Rogers. Likely as not, especially if guests arrive, he will be up late into the night playing like there was no tomorrow but still be ready early the next morning for a day's work.

In our time, Frankie McWhorter is an open window not only to the collective memories of his mentors, but to the knowledge they no doubt possessed of fiddlers from the 19th century. Through Frankie's memory, Wills (b. 1905), Robertson (b. 1897), and Rogers (b. 1895) represent a path to the past that can still be traveled. His regard for the legacy they passed on to him is exceeded only by the care he has taken to preserve it. "Cattle in the Cane," "Tommy Don't Go," "Hoppin' Lucy," or something as simple as "Varsouviana" in the hands of Frankie McWhorter are more than fiddle tunes. His performance traverses decades of life on the Texas Panhandle and the spirit of its people.

[Recent CD/cassette releases of *The Ranch Dance Fiddle: Frankie McWhorter* and *Texas Sandman: Frankie McWhorter* are available from Fiel Publications, 3716-27th Street, Lubbock, Texas 79410, (806) 791-3967. A re-release of the book *Cowboy Fiddler in Bob Wills' Band* by Frankie McWhorter as told by John Erickson is available from University of North Texas Press, (800) 826-8911. For more information on Frankie McWhorter visit http://www.ranchdance.com online]

Tommy Don't Go

For triple fiddles. Arrangement by Frankie McWhorter; transcribed by Lanny Fiel. ©1997 Elnora Music.
From the recording *Ranch Dance Fiddle: Frankie McWhorter.*

Bruce Molsky: Tradition and Individuality in Old Time Music

By Mary Larsen

One of today's most gifted and most popular old time fiddlers, multi-instrumentalist Bruce Molsky has devoted much of his life to the traditional music of southern Appalachia. Bruce was born in New York City, but moved to Virginia in the late 1970s to be closer to the music he had grown to love. Formerly a mechanical engineer by trade, Bruce has recently embarked on a full-time career in music and is busier than ever — teaching workshops, recording, writing, and performing. Over the years, Bruce has played in such venues as the Smithsonian Institution, Lincoln Center, the Clearwater, Live Oak, and Wheatland music festivals, as well as at countless workshops and contests. In 1997, he appeared on Garrison Keillor's "A Prairie Home Companion" with his group Big Hoedown. He also performs solo and with his wife Audrey.

How did you get interested in old time music?

A series of coincidences. When I was a teenager I wanted to be a bluegrass guitar player. I played some bluegrass in New York when I was growing up. And the first time I went to college, in Ithaca, I tried to hook up with some people, and looked for a bluegrass fiddler to play with. I found a fiddler, but I didn't know he was an old time and not a bluegrass fiddler. One thing led to another. We played all these cool tunes, and the next thing I knew I wanted to learn to play the fiddle. That was 1972. And I started tagging along to all the fiddlers' conventions in the summertime. By 1976 I had just uprooted and moved to the South.

How did you hook up with Tommy Jarrell?

I met Tommy Jarrell at his house. I was staying with a friend near Mt. Airy — Tommy lived in Toast, right close by. My friend dropped me off at Tommy's house while he went to do some grocery shopping, and his car broke down, and of course, Tommy didn't have a phone. So there was no way for him to get in touch. I ended up spending the whole day there, just playing music. Tommy was a really engaging, nice guy. Just a nice man. He loved people. I'd been playing fiddle for about a year at that point, and he just said, "Well, let's play together," which scared me to death. Then he told me, "Stop doing that, do this." He wasn't what you might call a music teacher, but he heard everything I was doing and he was very happy to tell me what I wasn't doing right. That's where I learned to play the fiddle — that one day, just hanging out with him. I had no idea how important that experience would be to me years later…I used to go visit him whenever I could after that.

How about Albert Hash?

When I lived in southwest Virginia in 1976, there were a bunch of people there that I played music with and they knew him from festivals. Some of us used to make little trips up to his house, kind of *en masse,* in these old Volkswagen bugs and pickup trucks, going up the side of Whitetop Mountain to see Albert. And I got to play with him a few times. He was also a really nice guy. He'd been around. I got to play head to head with him, and just watch him.

…All these old guys, they all played their own way, and here we come along one or two generations later and study each rendition like it's the definitive way the tune goes. But in truth it's not the "correct" version, just the way this individual player played it. I've always based my playing on old-fashioned renditions, but I also think there's always a danger of getting bogged down in reverence by saying that you should only play something a certain way because so-and-so did it that way. It's more important to understand what that person did, and how they did it. That way, you've got a baseline understanding of the tune when you choose to change or embellish it. You can see the differences much more clearly…I've listened to a lot of eastern Kentucky music, including most of the archival recordings that Lomax made in the '30s. Many of those players lived in pretty close proximity to each other, and I imagine many of them knew each other. Yet they all played tunes differently…

Listening to John Salyer was really eye-opening for me, because he played many of the same tunes as Bill Stepp and Luther Strong, but boy, he was not afraid to add beats and twist parts around and change them. I've got a little theory that I think these fiddlers did that on purpose. I think they took a tune and to kind of make a signature out of it, they might purposely change it. John Hartford and Bob Carlin have been working with all these old Ed Haley recordings, and Ed Haley recorded, for example, "Hell Among the Yearlings," a common

"Listen to music from every possible angle. Listen for syncopation, listen for tonality, listen to it by comparing it to other things… Make believe you're a dancer and listen to it like you want to dance to it…."

tune a lot of people play. But he also recorded a phenomenal, beautiful variation of it, called "Wild Ox in the Mud," all changed around, so I guess that's kind of his creative embellishment. John Salyer did the same thing. He played "Lost Girl," a fairly common tune, and then he played "Lost Boy." "Lost Boy" is pretty much "Lost Girl," but with the first part being in 9-time instead of 8. Maybe these were contest pieces, I don't know.

Who are some of your favorite old time fiddlers, past and present, aside from the ones you've just mentioned?

I should have made a list. There are just so many. Like the Round Peak fiddlers — the Virginia, North Carolina fiddlers — there's Tommy [Jarrell], of course. Fred Cockerham, too. Fred was an unsung rock and roll hero, and his playing was so syncopated and powerful. And many others from around there, like Ernest East and Benton Flippen. I met Robert Sykes a few times. He had a very bluesy style. And I've always been a big fan of Norman Edmonds' playing. He was a great dance fiddler.

One of my favorite fiddlers in the context of a band is John Lusk of Tennessee. He played with Murph Gribble and Albert York. They were recorded for the AFS [Archive of Folk Song, Library of Congress] in the 1940s. That band was the most interactive three musicians I've ever heard. That's something that I place a very high value on, being interactive with other people while you're playing. The very best band music you can hear happens when the players are listening to each other instead of to themselves.

Are there any types of music you like to listen to other than old time?

Yeah, I even play some other kinds of music. I've been a jazz buff since I was a teenager. I hack away at it a little bit on the guitar, but have always followed it fairly seriously, especially bebop and the more modern jazz forms… I also like some rock music, and I've always been a big R&B and Motown fan, having grown up in New York. That never went away. I don't know how much that affects how I play old time music, but I know it does…When I first learned to play old time music — I guess this has to happen, when you really, really want to learn something — I felt like it had to be to the exclusion of all the other music styles around. So many people define themselves by the kind of music that they play or the kind that they listen to. It's such a social experience. And when I first discovered old time music, I didn't want to hear anything else. Nothing else was important. I was never going to get a grip of this tangible element, this thing, this sound these old players had. So I had to forsake everything else, and I did for a long time. But in retrospect it was more of an intellectual exercise. I eventually realized that you are who you are, and music doesn't make you into anyone else. You can't fool anybody with it.

Do you have any tips or advice for fiddlers — beginners and more advanced ones?

The same advice applies to both of them. At the risk of sounding trite: just listen. Listen to everything you can listen to. Listen to music from every possible angle. Listen for syncopation, listen for tonality, listen to it by comparing it to other things. Old time music is this incredible stew of so many different kinds of music. Listen to the blues in southern music, to the bluesy notes and rhythms. Make believe you're a dancer and listen to it like you want to dance to it. And learn to identify all those elements when you listen. As an engineer, I'm pretty analytical about it, but I think anything complex can be better understood when it's broken down into its elements. Old time music is no exception. I teach workshops the same way — we go a piece at a time and then just weave the pieces together. I guess specifically for beginning fiddlers, there are several challenges. One is to of course learn the mechanics of the instrument, but the other is to learn what the music *feels* like, which I think is something people have the hardest time with. And I do, too. When they hear an old time tune, or any kind of music, they say, "That's not old-timey sounding," or "That is old-timey sounding." Then you ask them, "Well, what makes that old-timey sounding? Is it the scratchy sound because it happened to be on a 78, or is it the regional accent of the person that's singing the song? What is it about it?" This drove me crazy for years.

Part of what I listen for when I'm learning a piece is the general mood and what in the music creates that mood. I'll put music in the cassette player, and listen to the same tune over and over and over again, until I can identify that certain feeling or setting. Hearing and understanding the old-fashioned musical scale is also extremely important. That element differentiates a lot of the older players' playing from what you hear today, because we all grew up with an evenly divided scale. I really like pushing the notes to the outside a little bit, and for that reason I like Swedish fiddling, because it's all over the place and takes so many freedoms with pitch. And that raises the question: if you listen to some of these quarter tones, micro tones, so much that they sound perfectly normal, then that kind of throws the whole thing up in the air as to whether there is a real "correct" scale. It forces you to trust your musical judgement instead of depending on the rules to tell you what's right and wrong.

Is there anything you'd like to add?

Just a word for fiddlers who feel like they are stuck sometimes, like their music isn't progressing or improving: don't give up! Find new things to work on, different tunes or tunings or techniques, or new folks to play with. A calculated change will almost always get you unstuck! The fiddle may be painfully unforgiving some days, but you know it's magical and uplifting others. Keep playing and listening and learning, and the rewards will always be there.

Discography

Feature Albums:
- *Lost Boy* (Rounder Records 0361, 1996)
- *Warring Cats* (Yodel-Ay-Hee 011, 1993)

Bruce Molsky & Big Hoedown
(Bruce Molsky, Beverly Smith, Rafe Stefanini):
- *Bruce Molsky and Big Hoedown* (Rounder 0421, 1997)

Collaborations:
- *Unicorn* (with Hesperus) (Dorian 80157, 1997)
- *Hush My Restless Soul* (with Carla Gover) (June Appal 0072, 1995)
- *The Hellbenders* (Carryon 0004, 1990)

- *Take Me As I Am* (With Bob Carlin) (Marimac 9023, 1989)
- *Old Time Music Dance Party* (A. Robic and the Exertions with Mike Seeger, Paul Brown & others) (Flying Fish 415, 1987)

Anthologies:
- *Banging and Sawing* (with Bob Carlin) (Rounder 0331, 1996)
- *Tribute to The Appalachian String Band Music Festival* (Chubby Dragon CD 1001, 1995)
- *The Young Fogies, Volume II* (Rounder 0369, 1995)
- *Third Annual Farewell Reunion*, (with Mike Seeger and The L-7s) (Rounder 0313, 1994)

- *Old Time Music on the Air* (Rounder 0331, 1994)
- *A Tribute to Tommy Jarrell* (Heritage Records 056, 1986)
- *Through the Ears,* (The Green Grass Cloggers) (Rounder 0228, 1986)
- *The Young Fogies* (Heritage Records 063, 1985)
- *Visits* (Heritage Records XXXIII, 1981)

Instructional Cassette: *Southern Old Time Fiddle Tour with Bruce Molsky*

Contact Bruce for information on bookings, recordings or workshops at 227 N. Greenbrier St., Arlington, VA 22203; (703) 276-9899; Fax: 703-276-9112; bruce.molsky@ibm.net

Buffalo Girls

From John Hatcher, transcribed by Jack Tuttle as played by Bruce Molsky on his *Lost Boy* album (Rounder 0361).
"Buffalo Girls" (no relation to "Buffalo Gals"), is played in AEAE tuning. It's played at a moderate tempo with a bouncy feel. The bowing is a close approximation, but feel free to make adjustments. — Jack Tuttle

Juan Reynoso: Hotlands Legend Carries on Dying Tradition

By Lindajoy Fenley

Photo: Tomás Casademunt, courtesy Discos Corason

Juan Reynoso's bowing is as good as ever, his hearing is sharper than a cactus thorn, and his musical memory is completely intact. This Mexican fiddle virtuoso says he feels like a teenager when he plays. Even so, at 86 he worries about what will happen to his music when he is gone.

Reynoso, a living legend known as the Paganini of the Hotlands, stands alone as the pillar of *Calentana* (Hotlands) music, carrying on a dying tradition with his incredibly extensive repertoire of *sones, gustos*, foxtrots, *pasodobles*, waltzes and marches, all of them only inside his head. He has never written down any of his compositions. In fact, he does not know how to read musical notation at all. Self-taught in every aspect of life and without any formal schooling, he learned to read words once he was an adult.

The traditional music of *Tierra Caliente* – a sweltering area spanning out from the Balsa River Basin of Southwestern Mexico – focuses on the fiddle with backup from a guitar or two and a *tamborita* (a small wooden drum). Today, guitarists use a normal, Spanish six-string instrument. But in *don*[1] Juan's early years as a musician in the wake of the 1910-1920 Mexican Revolution, accompanists played the *guitarra panzona*. This short, thick-bodied guitar provided *obligados*, or melodic bass lines, as well as chords that were pounded as much as they were strummed.

One reason Calentana music has not received much attention for decades is that younger musicians from the region prefer the driving tropical sounds of their electric guitars, snare sets and synthesizers. The homogenized music they play brings in more money than the many traditional styles from Mexico's myriad of cultural regions. Most of the few remaining traditional musicians who have stuck with what don Juan calls "the music of yesteryear" are also older men. A couple of months ago – just a week before 94-year-old fiddler Filiberto Salmerón of nearby Tlapehuala, Guerrero, died – don Juan reminisced about his former friends and rivals who made the traditional Tierra Caliente music come alive at informal *cantina* gatherings and fancy parties long ago.

First, he recalled his mentor, Isaías Salmerón, a local violinist and composer who showed him how to play the guitarra panzona and the fiddle when he was just a boy. Isaías, who composed a major portion of the region's traditional repertoire, has been dead since 1942. "Don Isaías Salmerón has left us. Juan Bartolo Tavira is gone. Then there were the other Tavira boys, like Angel Tavira, the one who plays fiddle without his right hand. He could go, too. Also don Remigio Rentería of Cutzamala was good… Don Leobardo El Hueso… (and) the guy from Tlapehuala…whose skin was all spotted and who wore pants with suspenders, good shoes, rings, gold chains… His name was Ignacio Rivera."

Don Juan also often remembers his best accompanists who have since died natural or violent deaths: Salomón Trujillo, a blind guitar player, Epifanio Avellaneda who played a mean tamborita, Juan Gallardo, an itinerant fiddler who lived at his house for five years, and his own son, Maximino Reynoso, a great singer and guitar player.

While most other Calentana groups include two fiddles, don Juan rarely plays with other fiddlers. Gallardo was an exception. He taught don Juan classical pieces like *Czardas* in exchange for learning the Calentana repertoire. Gallardo would play the first while Juan's fingers would dance above and below the melody line, harmonizing with his violin.

Just because Juan can't read or write music does not mean he doesn't understand musical theory. His understanding is innate; it isn't intellectualized. He simply enjoys creating complex harmonies when given the chance. When his is the only fiddle, he double stops practically every note. He can play harmony on his instrument while singing melody. He also works out the harmonies his sons play on their guitars when they accompany him.

In the first half of the century, don Juan's type of music was extremely popular throughout Tierra Caliente. There were string bands of four and five musicians playing *sones* and *gustos* with violins, guitars and tamboritas, and orchestras with both stringed and wind instruments. These groups were in demand for weddings, baptisms, wakes and all other sorts of social and political gatherings. Today, there are just a few groups that play *música de arrastre* or *música de cuerda* as the regional style is sometimes called locally. But led by

---

[1] *Don* is a respectful title frequently used in Spanish-speaking countries; it is not part of the names of the fiddlers referred to in this article.

"The first year he went to the Festival of American Fiddle Tunes, he was amazed to see so many musicians gathered in one place, making music inside the buildings and outside on the lawns, day and night... 'You throw out a lasso and wherever it falls, it lands on a musician,' he told people back home."

"the Paganini of the Hotlands," the *Conjunto de Juan Reynoso* is undoubtedly the best. Oldtimers remember people used to say, "It's going to be a good wedding; Juan Reynoso is going to play!"...

In the past year, don Juan has been getting quite a bit of attention and is beginning to believe the music of Tierra Caliente will survive. Perhaps the thundering applause he received at the Festival of American Fiddle Tunes in Port Townsend, Washington, in 1996 and 1997 reached Mexico City. His international acclaim, combined with his dedicated masterful musical ability displayed in Mexico for seven decades, inspired the Mexican government last year to honor him with the National Prize for Science and Arts. It is the highest national honor an artist can receive in Mexico.

Don Juan likes to play his violin more than anything else. He also enjoys making up nicknames for people and talking in the sayings country people use to describe their world. He makes up his own sayings or at least finds a new use for ones he has heard in another context. The first year he went to the Festival of American Fiddle Tunes, he was amazed to see so many musicians gathered in one place, making music inside the buildings and outside on the lawns, day and night. He also remarked about the "unusual" number of female musicians, which would not be common in Mexico. "You throw out a lasso and wherever it falls, it lands on a musician," he told people back home.

None of don Juan's numerous children have taken up the fiddle although he has taught at least four sons to accompany him on the guitar. While he is proud of their talent, he likes to boast that he has more *joie de vivre* than all of them put together. "Next to me, my sons are a couple of old grandfathers," he says every now and then....

Although don Juan lurches to the right because a painful leg forces him to take slow, measured steps, he still likes to hike into town and play in bars and restaurants with a faithful accompanist, Cástulo Benitez de la Paz. When he tires, he sometimes stops inside the Altamirano Cathedral to cool off from the 100-degree heat. There, in the empty sanctuary and in the quiet of the afternoon, he opens his fiddle case and plays for a special audience. He plays for God and the saints.

He is one of the very few musicians to play inside the main church that way. But he has plenty of company in a chapel across town every November 22 when musicians gather to play for their patron saint, Santa Cecilia. At these and other gatherings, as well as when he is alone, don Juan plays because the music transports him. The music he plays keeps him young; it keeps him alive.

The question is: how will this music live on once El Maestro Juan has joined the other great musicians he likes to reminisce about?

Discography

Juan Reynoso with Neyo and Javier Reynoso, Live at the Festival of American Fiddle Tunes, Volumes 1-4 (newly released recordings from Swing Cat Productions, P.O. Box 30153, Seattle, WA 98103; (206) 440-1844; http://www.w-link.net/~panastasio/):

• *Volume One: On Fire and In Concert* (Swing Cat #CD 1507)
• *Volume Two: Hot as Habenero* (Swing Cat #CD 1508)
• *Volume Three: Viva Tierra Caliente* (Swing Cat #CD 1509)
• *Volume Four: With Passion* (Swing Cat #CD 1510)

• *Juan Reynoso: El Paganini de la Tierra Caliente interpreta sones y gustos* (Discos Corason)
• *Antologia del Son* (Música Tradicional)

• *Juan Reynoso: Son, Gusto, PasoDoble, Fox, Vals de Tierra Caliente* (Pentagrama)
• *Juan Reynoso: El Paganini de la Sierra y su Conjunto regional* (Discos del Balsas)
• *Juan Reynoso, El Virtuoso del Violín* (Astro Discos)
• *Juan Reynoso y su conjunto regional* (Producciones Guerrero)
• *Juan Reynoso, Sones y Gustos de Tierra Caliente 15 éxitos* (Astro Discos)
• *Canto a Guerrero con el Conjunto Hermanos Mondragón y el violín de Juan Reynoso* (Orbe)
• *V Encuentro de Cantores del Pueblo de Guerrero* (CBS)
• *Conjunto Juan Reynoso – Música Tradicional de la Región de Tierra Caliente* (Universidad Autónomo de Guerrero)

The *Encuentro de Dos Tradiciones Musicales* (Encounter of Two Musical Traditions) honoring Juan Reynoso brings together traditional musicians from both sides of the border. Just before the third annual event in February 1999, Dos Tradiciones, A.C. was established as a non-profit organization in Mexico to ensure the continuation of this festival as well as other related events. Lindajoy Fenley, who can provide information about Dos Tradiciones' cultural exchange programs in Mexico, can be contacted at (011 525) 271-3430 and (011 525) 273-4979 or by email at lindajoy@ laneta.apc. org. Information is also available on the web at http://www.laneta.apc.org/Dostradiciones.

Ninfa

Transcribed by Paul Anastasio as played by Juan Reynoso on Vol. 3 of Swing Cat's Juan Reynoso series: *Viva Tierra Caliente*.

Dale Russ: Irish Fiddling on the Pacific Rim

By Larry Hill

Dale Russ is a friendly, unassuming man who plays Irish traditional music with distinctive clarity, articulation, and soul. Born in the U.S., he picked up the fiddle as a young adult in Washington state, far from the urban Irish enclaves. Yet, in 1993, Martin Hayes told Folk World magazine, "Dale Russ...is one of the greatest fiddlers I know in Irish traditional music..." Recognized by such luminaries as Kevin Burke, Liz Carroll, and James Kelly, Dale plays music for dancing, for listening, and for pleasure, mostly in the Pacific Northwest. He plays with the Suffering Gaels and with Jody's Heaven. He also performs solo and has toured in Japan to enthusiastic audiences... He has taught Irish fiddling at the Lark In The Morning Music Camp, at the Festival of American Fiddle Tunes, and at the Swannanoa Gathering. He also teaches privately and in workshops and on video. Subtle, inventive, and steeped in the tradition, his intense work ethic and concentration are matched only by the sheer joyfulness of his music. We spoke during the Northwest Folklife festival in May 1996, where Dale performed in four separate venues in a single day.

How did you come to the fiddle and to Irish music, and did you do it at the same time?

I didn't play Irish music before I played the fiddle, and I only picked up the fiddle when I moved out to Olympia (Washington) in 1973. There was a bunch of people who were all learning how to play at the same time, so we kind of taught each other the little bits of information we knew. I was playing the guitar in a bluegrass band, messing around with bluegrass, really a mishmash of stuff, a few old timey tunes, a few Scottish, a few Irish, a few contra dance...It was a consortium of beginners. The only established fiddle player I knew who was playing anything vaguely Irish or Scottish was Frank Ferrel. He was living in Seattle and had his fiddle shop going at that time. He played Irish and Scots tunes, but he didn't play them in a strictly Irish style. When it came to learning Irish music, we'd pick up techniques from people coming back from Ireland, from people who had gone over to learn.

So there was no one in particular who guided you in Irish music or on the fiddle. You made your own way.

I think somebody showed me how to do bowed triplets somewhere in there. There was a teach-in I saw in *Sing Out!* magazine where Aly Bain explained how to play "turns" — rolls. From there, I realized what I was hearing on the records of like, Jean Carignan. I had a Martin Byrnes recording, but ironically he doesn't play rolls. I only found that out years later by listening more carefully. Basically, it was all studying on my own, from recordings of whoever I could get...Somebody brought back a tape of Paddy Glackin at some session...There was Paddy on one side and Brendan McGlinchey on the other, so I took those from the cassette player and put them on reel to reel and slowed them down to half speed.

Looking back, is there anything you would do differently that would make the whole process easier or more productive?

In terms of technique, there wasn't a whole lot of dead time. There were some bowing things that took me a while to catch on to, but I think, like a lot of things, when I was ready for it, there it was. I heard it, and I was able to figure out what was going on. I really was flying blind for a long time, but occasionally someone would come through town, or I'd get some kind of confirmation that what I was doing was the right thing, that I was on the right track. If someone else was around that knew what was going on, that could have given me that affirmation earlier on, I'd probably be a more confident player than I am. Because the rest of it was just work, just getting the techniques.

You played a lot of dances then, and you still do...

When I first started with that same group at Evergreen [College], we put together a Thursday night contra dance, or square dance, or whatever kind of dance people were doing. It was a group situation where I got to play tunes up to speed. It was invaluable to be able to play loud and to know that no one was going to hear your mistakes. That was really, really useful. I also started playing for *Feises*, as early as 1978 or 1979, and playing for step dancers was also really valuable. To watch the motion, to watch the dances being done and to see physically the way the bodies move to execute the steps really helped with rhythm and phrasing. [And], I really enjoy playing for an old style step dancer. Solo, hard shoe, reel, jig, hornpipe — old style, I love that. I really enjoy the interplay, rhythmically. When I was a kid

"I love rhythm. So, really, I think of the bow as a drumstick with hair on it."

the first instrument I wanted to play was drums, and there's still that desire in me for rhythm. I love rhythm. So, really, I think of the bow as a drumstick with hair on it.

During your learning phases, what was your methodology, or did you just pile on the tunes?

When I was first learning there were as many tunes that I wanted to learn as I could fit in. There were always new tunes to learn. I had basic technique — again, triplets and rolls — but I had to learn those at a very slow pace and then bring them up to speed, so I invented exercises to enable me to do that. It is kind of a painstaking process that is ongoing.

You mean small muscle coordination.

Yes. You have to train yourself to be able to do that, but it's well worth the effort. [For instance], I've got a little finger exercise I like to do, for getting my fourth finger to work, you know, to get it part of the family. Get your hand positioned on the A string for playing a major scale. Play jig time: AEE, BEE, C#EE, DEE, C#EE, BEE, AEE, making sure your E is in tune with the open string. You don't have to play unison, but make sure it is there. Then, after you've played the major scale, change the C sharp to a C natural, and do it in a minor key. You don't have to do it for very long before your hand starts to cramp. Stop, do it again until your hand starts to cramp, stop. Do that every day, or every other day, for a few minutes. For people who want to include the little finger — the feeling for me was okay, there is the first, second, and third finger. Then there is the little guy on the end who doesn't know what to do, or can't do it. The feeling for me was getting these four guys to all be part of the family. I think for people who want to be more effective, that's a good place to start.

We've been talking about left hand techniques, and about the bow as an instrument of rhythm, but how do we find the soul of Irish music?

The short answer is, listen. There is not necessarily a feeling that is uniquely Irish because the Irish people have the same feelings as every other people. You are talking about basic emotions within a certain linguistic context. Recently, I've been trying to learn a little Japanese, and I want to know, what is it that constitutes a Japanese accent? I try to speak it, but there is still something that I'm not quite getting. When I was learning how to play, I had to make this conscious choice at one point whether I was going to play bluegrass fiddle or Irish fiddle. One thing that I noticed was that I didn't have any problem making my fiddle sound "bluegrass," but I couldn't make it sound "Irish." I realized, I've been listening to bluegrass music for years, country music since I was a kid, so I was familiar with it, and it was an easy thing to reproduce in my head. So I figured what I needed to do was listen to Irish music all the time. I constantly had it on the turntable or tape recorder so that I would become familiar with that accent. Part of the learning process was to actually have the music slowed down so I could hear it, and analyze it, and I would practice at the same half speed I was hearing it. Then I'd bring it up to speed, gradually.

Do you have any parting advice for people starting out in this music?

You listen a lot and be patient. You realize that a lot of technique, making it sound Irish, is going to take time. I don't have a lot of regular students, I think because a lot of people come in and then they realize how much work it is going to take to sound the way they want to sound. Like they didn't understand that they're really going to have to work to play this kind of music. I tell people you don't have to play rolls or triplets to play Irish music. The ornaments are only part of it. You can still play beautiful Irish music without having any ornamentation. Be patient, be willing to take the time.

Notes to the transcription: Try tuning your G string down one half-step to F#. This will allow you to get the low note transcribed in lines 3, 7, and 9, measure 1. The very first three notes of the tune (F#, F natural, F#) are all played with the second finger and on one bow stroke. Bowing notation is minimal, indicating only those cases which seemed important. Please do not assume that notes are single bowed where there is no notation.

Discography

• *Garden of Butterflies,* Jody's Heaven, Aniar Records, 1998
• *Reeds and Rosin,* with Todd Denman, Aniar Records, 1998
• *Jody's Heaven,* Aniar Records, 1996 (originally Foxglove Records)
• *Dale Russ: Irish Fiddle,* Aniar Records (originally Foxglove Records 1995)

• *The One Horned Cow,* The Suffering Gaels, Foxglove Records, 1996
• *'bout time,* The Suffering Gaels, independent, 1990.
• *The Boston College Irish Fiddle Festival, My Love is in America,* Green Linnet, 1990 [43 Beaver Brook Rd., Danbury, CT, 06810]
• *The 1983 Northwest Folklife Festival, Vol. V,* Northwest Folklife, one track with Mike Saunders.

Instructional Video:
• *Basic Irish Fiddle,* Lark in the Morning, 1986

For bookings, lessons, or information on recordings/video, Dale may be contacted at 8620 18th Ave. SW, Seattle, WA 98106, (206) 768-1511; Email: russ@sttl.uswest.net

Aniar Records, P.O. Box 210481, San Francisco, CA 94121, (415) 759-8370; www.aniar.com

February Reel #1

By Dale Russ. Transcribed by Dale from *Dale Russ: Irish Fiddle* (Aniar Records).

Oliver Schroer:
Busking Pays Off!

By Mary Larsen

Toronto fiddle player Oliver Schroer defies easy categorization. His 1993 album *Jigzup* (nominated for a JUNO award in the Roots/Traditional category), is an impressive collection of original tunes with a very traditional flavor, while his 1994 effort *Whirled* demonstrates his interests in jazz, improvisation, and world music. In addition to promoting his CDs and his bands "Big Ripping Band" and "The Stewed Tomatoes," Schroer is kept very busy as a session musician, sideman, producer, and composer. I had the opportunity to chat with him at the 1995 North American Folk Alliance Conference in Portland, Oregon.

Schroer started off with classical violin lessons at age eight. After a few years, however, he, like his teacher ("not a happy musician"), found himself getting bored. "But I loved to improvise, make up things. I didn't get the point of always playing the same thing... Nobody told me that improvising was something that you do, that you're allowed to do this. So it became a huge battle, and I quit when I was sixteen and got a guitar, and played [jazz and blues] guitar for ten years." During that time, he didn't touch the fiddle, aside from learning two fiddle tunes "on a bet." "I joined a country swing band in my late twenties and the band leader knew me from a long time ago, and knew that I had played these two fiddle tunes on a bet. We had to do a square dance, so I had to learn some more fiddle tunes. I was really, totally hooked. I began learning tunes, learning tunes, and just took off." Shortly thereafter, he began "busking," playing on the street as part of Toronto's official subway busking program. He started with a repertoire of thirty-five tunes, mostly traditional Canadian, gradually adding French-Canadian, Scottish, Swedish, Norwegian, Balkan... "I just kept moving East. Then I studied Indian violin for awhile. Meanwhile, my tastes were still pretty eclectic. I listened to everything from jazz to country to blues, to fusion. I began hearing a certain kind of fiddle tune in my head that I couldn't find anywhere, so I began making them up." When he started working on his albums, he had a decision to make. "I thought, am I going to do an album with more jigs and reels, more 4/4, 6/8 stuff? Or am I going to do an album with really wild things — more multimedia things, and strange things that I've written... I thought it would be better to keep things in one vein and move on to the next thing. So I decided to split them up, and I didn't know what I was getting into. I began recording both albums simultaneously. The master tapes are a couple of tunes from one album, a couple from the next album...all mixed up. I did that over the next three years or so. I ate a lot of potatoes doing those albums. Finally we released *Jigzup* in November of 1993, and six weeks later it got nominated for a JUNO award. That was a very good break for me."

Asked which style of music he prefers to play, Schroer said, "I love traditional music. I do a whole range of stuff. I still play contra dances with a band that I work with, and I play acoustic fiddle. But for myself, it's probably the wilder stuff. I've done a lot of writing over the last six months and I'm trying to balance out the repertoire so that there's a real mix of stuff. My girlfriend is a fiddle player who started just four years ago, but she is really in love with Cajun music, so I hear a lot of that. I'm finding that the stuff I've been writing lately is being a little Cajun blues-inflected."

"I sometimes describe myself as a musical filter or sieve — a lot of stuff goes in, and gets conjugulated around, and then it comes out again as my tunes. So where I see it going is that there are some really wild things, and then there are some things that are more like jigs and reels, or blues, or Cajun-inflected things, so there's a real mix. When I was doing these albums, I wanted to do albums of fiddle music for the non-fiddler, as well as the fiddler. Because you know, fiddlers can listen to endless amounts of fiddle music, and it all sounds interesting, it's exciting...but non-fiddlers will last for about three tunes. I wanted to make an album that could be listened to, front to back, by people who have no experience with fiddle music — to contemporize it without trivializing it, without adding gratuitous bells and whistles."

But performing is what Schroer most enjoys. "The whole thing about an audience that sits and listens, I really like. I tell a lot of stories... A lot of my tunes have wacky titles, and they usually end up being the punchline of a story. I'll tell a story, and draw people out — it's like having lyrics, it engages people's minds, and then they listen to the music, and it engages people's musical sense. It goes back and forth like that."

Schroer's plans for the next couple of years are possibly more eclectic and ambitious than his past efforts. With his band The Stewed Tomatoes he plans another album which he describes as "quite a different experience." He also plans an acoustic album with Vermont fiddler Pete Sutherland and Keith Murphy on guitar and piano. He is also working on an album of hymns and an album of circus music.

"I sometimes describe myself as a musical filter or sieve — a lot of stuff goes in, and gets conjugulated around, and then it comes out again as my tunes."

Parting comments: "When I was playing in the subway back when I started out, I felt like I was stupidly stubborn — I wasn't going to give up, I wasn't going to stop doing it because I really loved playing the fiddle, but I just didn't know where it was taking me. I'm astounded where it's taken me a few years later — that I'm getting the chance to do all this stuff, that I've got these albums that I'm very happy about, that it's taken me this far. I feel blessed — this is such an amazing thing to be able to do this. I just want to be able to keep doing it."

Afterward: Since this interview was conducted in 1995, Oliver has been busy composing, playing his fiddle, and producing. After *Stewed Tomatoes,* he released *Celtica,* an album of his compositions, on the Avalon label. Avalon also released his Juno-nominated *Celtic Dance.* He is currently on the verge of releasing a new double CD of original unaccompanied solo violin/fiddle pieces. The album will be called *O2* and the tunes draw from such diverse sources as traditional airs, Norwegian fiddle music, Creole blues (e.g. Calvin Carrière and Canray Fontenot) and Bach partitas. Other upcoming projects include a solo tour, a new Stewed Tomatoes CD, two new discs of quartettes and trios, and a collaboration with some French Canadian musicians. And Oliver was recently announced as one of four composers commissioned to write music for Canada Day Celebrations in the year 2000 at Harbourfront, Ontario.

Oliver's playing appears on over 75 albums of new traditional, new acoustic, and pop music. Some recent recording highlights include album sessions with American songwriting legends Jimmy Webb and Barry Mann, Canadian female country supergroup Quartette, and Newfoundland "alterna-trad" rockers Great Big Sea. He is also a busy producer, most recently for James Keelaghan (*Road*) and Holmes Hooke (*Caught by the Tale*). Four of his productions have been nominated for a Canadian Juno award: in 1998, Teresa Doyle's *If Fish Could Sing* and his own *Celtic Dance* (Avalon); in 1997, Thomas Handy's *Arc*; and in 1993, his own *Jigzup.*

Oliver frequently plays with The Stewed Tomatoes and other groups, and he has recently been gaining more prominence as a solo performer. Some recent solo playing highlights have been a CBC broadcast concert at the Northern Encounters Festival in Toronto, and a show at the Lincoln Center in New York.

Discography

- *Oliver Schroer and The Stewed Tomatoes,* Big Dog Music, 1997
- *Jigzup,* Big Dog Music, 1993
- *Whirled,* Big Dog Music, 1994

For information on bookings or to order Oliver's CDs, contact him at 589 Markham St., Toronto, Ontario, Canada M6G 2L7. (Phone: (416) 516-4806.) Transcriptions of all the tunes on *Jigzup* are also available, as well as a book of jigs, reels, and waltzes.]

Horseshoes & Rainbows

By Oliver Schroer. Transcribed by Oliver Schroer as played on *Jigzup.*

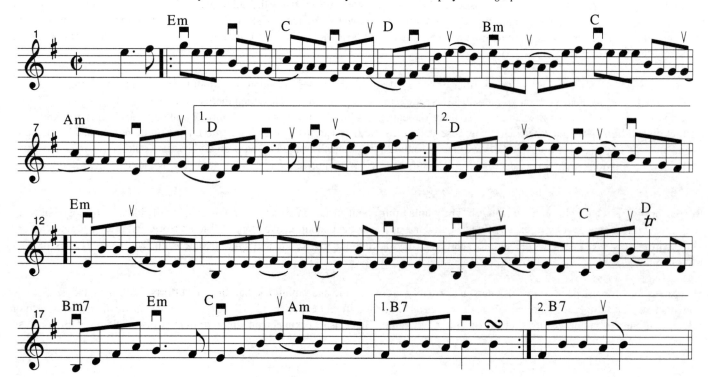

Pierre Schryer:
Legendary Canadian Fiddler

By Charlie Walden

Canadian old-time fiddling has always fascinated me. The tradition shares many similarities to the music of my native Missouri: The playing style emphasizes clean, well-articulated bowing; Canadian hoe-downs and reels are "notey," melodically complex and played with drive suitable for square dancing; Canadians embrace other tune types in their repertoire, such as jigs, hornpipes, polkas, and waltzes.

Over the past decade the name Schryer has become unalterably associated with the best of Canadian fiddling. Certainly Julien Schryer and Juliette Audet of Sault Ste. Marie ("the Soo" for short), Ontario, could never have imagined the success their progeny would attain. Their first son, Patrick, was a guitarist, followed by Raymond, who became a fiddler and initially patterned his playing after his uncle Bud Schryer.

In case of the fiddling Schryers, good things come in sets of three, namely the fiddling Schryer triplets — Louis, Pierre and Dan — who were born in 1968. All three along with older brother Raymond and sister Julie on piano have enjoyed undisputed domination of competitive fiddling in Canada for twenty years. Their accomplishment in winning major Canadian fiddling competitions amounted to nothing short of dynasty in the early 1980s through the late 1990s.

They imitated and mastered the styles of the greatest Canadian fiddlers ever known, such as Graham Townsend, Ward Allen, Don Messer, and Jean Carignan. They also followed closely the music of Sean McGuire of Ireland, Jerry Holland of Cape Breton, and Americans Bobby Hicks, Mark O'Connor and Johnny Gimble. The compact disc release by the Schryer triplets (*Triple Fiddle,* The Schryer Triplets, Canada, 1993) is a remarkable display of combined and individual mastery of fiddling and showcases these many influences. In recent years the triplets have set about to make their individual marks on the world of traditional music.

Pierre Schryer in particular has distinguished himself as a world class Celtic fiddler while still maintaining his Canadian roots. He worked for a time with older brother Raymond as a violin maker but has since set his tools aside in favor of a full-time career as a working musician. He has assembled a band which includes his sister Julie on piano, Brian Pickell on guitar, and multi-instrumentalist Nathan Curry, and is actively touring with this group in the company of step dancers of the Irish, Scottish and French-Canadian traditions.

Pierre's past activities include the release of a CD entitled *The New Canadian Waltz* (1996 New Canadian Records) which features his band along with percussionist Brad Fremlin, a tour with British Columbia-based Celtic-funk group Mad Pudding, and an Ireland tour in the spring of 1997 which included representing Canada in a fiddle showcase in Limerick. Pierre also excels as an illustrator, and has had numerous local showings of his artwork.

Were there any other fiddlers in your family? All your siblings are musicians, aren't they?

Yes, my oldest brother Patrick played guitar. There's my uncle, Bud Schryer. He played fiddle and was well known in the Sault Ste. Marie area. He was an old-time fiddler and admired people like Don Messer. He played for the dances here and was inducted into the fiddlers Hall of Fame. He provided a lot of good music for the people here, mainly for the square dances. Also, my dad recalls his father playing fiddle but I never got to hear him. My dad played guitar and used to sing to us when we were kids.

Who was your biggest influence when you were starting out?

That would have to be my older brother Raymond. He went off to school in Toronto and came back with some great tapes and records and let us use them and listen to them. I play a lot with Julie, my sister, these different styles of fiddling. Raymond introduced us to the different styles that were out there. He was into Irish, Scottish, Shetland, and he was bringing it all home — even some American stuff. Of course the real learning was happening with the triplets. We sort of bounced things off of each other. We all started at the same age; we were eight years old. We were classically trained at the same time we were going to fiddle contests. This went on through the time we were eighteen or so.

When the triplets were playing against each other, I guess you first had to compete against older brother Raymond.

No, not really. Raymond is seven years older than the rest of us so he was in a different category in the competitions.

" I believe session playing is a major thing. If a person can put himself or herself in that position, and absorb the music, the style and the atmosphere, that's the best way to learn."

So the triplets were competing against each other?

That's right. It was only in the later years that we played against Raymond. The triplets competed in the twelve and under category and went up through the different categories and then into the Open. We started into the Open as early as age sixteen. It was friendly rivalry.

That wasn't too common, was it?

No, but it's happening more and more. It seems like the young ones are learning really, really quick…There's so much access to CDs and tapes around, and teachers. They're all into it. They can get really good at twelve and compete in the Open at age fifteen or sixteen and do well.

Aspiring players always want to know what a good player such as yourself does to maintain your playing ability and to learn new tunes. What kind of routine do you use?

Basically, I try to practice when I'm in the mood. I want to accomplish as much as possible. It might be just a half hour or sometimes a spurt of three hours. If I'm in the mood to learn new tunes or need to learn new tunes, that's what I'll do. The other practices are dedicated to playing tunes I already know and trying to improvise or improve them. And certainly technique is always involved. I've always been concerned about the technique, my bowing, the feeling of the tune, and all that has to be practiced.

You guys (the triplets) play so much alike, the genetic connection is unmistakable. It's really remarkable.

I guess we don't realize that as much as people listening because we've played together so much over the years. It's like second nature for us.

In seeing you and Raymond play together here in Chicago a couple of years ago, it was entertaining to see you guys give signals to each other while you're playing and change things in the tunes on the fly. Very amazing to watch.

Yeah, we look at each other, give the glare. We definitely do the connection thing while we're playing. In the early years we didn't realize how much we rubbed off on each other. Now we see this. And of course, we've branched off from there, too. We can still go back to the triplet thing, but now we've branched off and done our own thing. We've found our own niche, I guess. Louis has gone more for the American style; I play more Celtic and Irish. Dan has stayed with the true Canadian style. But when we play together we still do the triplet thing or go our way and have something interesting happening. It's really satisfying.

When did you start playing the Irish music? That seems to be your main interest now.

I like all the different styles, but Irish was very strong when I was in Ottawa from '88 to '93. And I learned things at home from tapes, especially Sean McGuire. Raymond started collecting that stuff and Julie went to Ireland and met Sean McGuire and played with him in 1981. She brought back some material. Since then I've wanted to learn more of it. And I've listened to a lot of Michael Coleman recordings. When I was in Ottawa I went to the Irish pubs — Monday nights at Rasputin's. I'd meet up with some friends. That's where I met up with Nathan Curry, who is in my band now, and James Stephens, who helped produce my CD.

When I was growing up, I didn't hear other kinds of fiddle music around the Soo, only in our own home. There were out-of-town jam sessions and we'd go to ten or twelve contests in the summer. So that really helped us develop and grow in session playing and competing. I believe session playing is a major thing. If a person can put himself or herself in that position, and absorb the music, the style and the atmosphere, that's the best way to learn.

As opposed to learning off of tapes?

Well that's the second best. The other one would be music sheets. That's the third down the line. You can't learn style or atmosphere or anything else from that… It's like learning a language. If you want to learn French and you set yourself in Québec, you learn it more quickly that way.

Discography

• *Pierre Schryer & Dermot Byrne, 2 Worlds United* (New Canadian Records, 1999)
• *The New Canadian Waltz* (New Canadian Records, 1996)
• *Triple Fiddle* (The Schryer Triplets, 1993)
• *The Gathering, Various Artists* (Real World, 1997)

Please see Pierre's website for information on his touring schedule, recordings and art work: http://www.pierreschryer.com

Bookings: Mac's Music; contact: Robin MacIntyre, R.R. #1, Goulais River, Ontario, Canada P0S 1E0; Phone/fax: (705) 649-2880; Email: bellevue@soonet.ca

New Canadian Records, P.O. Box 20046, 150 Churchill Blvd., Sault Ste. Marie, Ontario, Canada P6A 6W3; Fax: (705) 246-0252

Order recordings directly from:
Elderly Instruments (USA): 517-372-7890, or Ottawa Folklore Centre (Canada): 1-800-385-3655.

The New Canadian Waltz

©Pierre Schryer, 1994. New Canadian Music, SOCAN. This is the title track of *The New Canadian Waltz* CD, recorded live.
A book with all the tunes transcribed from this CD will be available in fall 1999.

"It was not until after I came back from Mark O'Connor's first annual fiddle camp in Nashville that I was motivated to write this waltz. With the inspiration coming from listening and hearing the different sounds of fiddle playing, I began amalgamating the various styles into one piece — a 'wee bit' of Cape Breton, a little Irish and Scottish, a touch of American and a hint of Canadian. This melody with its blended cultural influences still feels very much Canadian, hence its title, 'The New Canadian Waltz.'" — Pierre Schryer

Björn Ståbi: Master Swedish Fiddler

By Patrice George

Björn Ståbi learned to fiddle as a child from his father in Stockholm, in the 1940s. His father, Erik, fiddled in the style of his native parish of Orsa, in the province of Dalarna. The tradition, in pre-industrial times, was for one or two fiddles to play unaccompanied. To enlarge the sound for weddings, processions, and other village occasions, the fiddlers developed a powerful language composed of arpeggios, ornaments, and stylized rhythms that commanded attention. Distinct forms of *polskas* (the most popular dance form in Sweden) developed within individual villages.

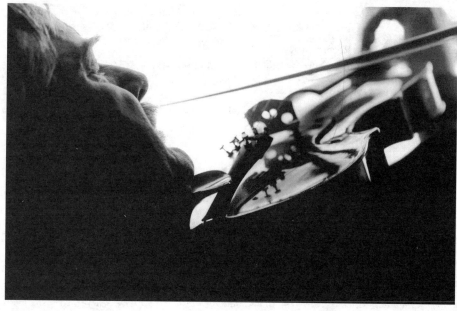

Photo: Thomas Fahlander

In the early 20th century, this old style of fiddling began to fade out, as the population moved from farms to towns. Urban workers preferred bands with accordions, which played more popular dances imported from continental Europe. Fiddling wasn't fashionable when Björn Ståbi was a child. However, many great fiddlers had moved to Stockholm to find jobs. Björn heard tunes from many different regions, by playing with both his father and the many friends who came to visit their home in Stockholm. Björn credits his mastery of playing "second" parts to the influence of Börtas Hans, a fiddler from Rättvik who came every week to play cards and fiddle with his father.

The Ståbi family returned each summer to the family homestead in Orsa, where Björn inherited the essence of Orsa music. Gössa Anders Andersson was his greatest influence, reflected in the style of his playing today: powerful, rhythmic, highly ornamented, shaded with "blue notes" or quarter tones that float between major and minor chords.

"Folk music should be fun," Ståbi mused, "or I wouldn't be in it!" He "speaks" with his fiddle and bow, and listens hard to what his playing partners are doing. "The best fiddling happens at night," he added, "when fiddlers get together to play just for the fun of it." Despite his traditional training, he has participated in many ensembles and projects that range from folk-rock to jazz to theatrical productions. He is also a painter and a woodworker, but the fiddle has been the center of his life's work.

Björn was one of the few young musicians who had learned first-hand from old rural fiddlers, when the folk revival era of the 1960s-'70s began. He was a leader in the folk movement, performing and teaching throughout Sweden. He was often featured on live Swedish radio and television folk music broadcasts, inspiring a huge growth of interest in traditional folk music throughout the country. When Björn was only twelve, he was performing on Swedish radio and caught the attention of Per Hans Olsson, who was ten at the time. Olsson was shocked that someone his age could sound so "old." The son of a fiddler as well, Per Hans also become a great fiddler (in the Rättvik tradition). He and Björn have been friends and collaborators since their teens, and have been recorded together many times. They generate fantastic energy when they play together. "We can't play at half speed," Ståbi wrote for their 1995 CD on Giga Records. "It's a matter of life and death!"

Pete Seeger invited Björn Ståbi and Ole Hjorth (another master fiddler) to perform at the Newport Folk Festival in 1969. "We had fifteen minutes on stage, between Arlo Guthrie and Johnny Cash," he remembers. That was the first time most folk music fans in this country had ever heard the fiddling of provincial Sweden. Since then, Björn has become one of the most active ambassadors for Swedish folk music, here and in Europe. He was invited back to tour the U.S. by the Smithsonian in 1974 and 1976.

In May 1997, Björn Ståbi came to New York City to play for a modern dance performance by Irene Hultman, a Swedish-born choreographer…He brought along the young fiddler Dan Sjöberg as well. They were invited to visit Scandia New York, a weekly folk dance class which meets at a synagogue in lower Manhattan. When Björn arrived he was quite surprised. "Is the devil welcome in here?" he asked, pointing to his fiddle case. Within a few minutes after Björn and Dan took the fiddles out of their cases, the devil would have had to flee anyway. The dancers were convinced that they had been transported to heaven. Björn and Dan were more than happy to let us local fiddlers join them. But we stood by in awe when they began to play regional polskas. It was an incredible privilege to have such fine musicians playing in Manhattan, as if it were a house party in Dalarna.

Björn and Dan returned the following week for a short fiddle workshop. Björn demonstrated the difference between polska styles in his home district of Orsa, and the district of Boda. "The rhythm of the polska follows the human heartbeat," Björn began. The basic structure is a 3/4 beat, with emphasis on the first and third beats. In Boda, the melody is played evenly, and the ornamentation is minimal. In Orsa, there is more of a pulse on the downbeat, and notes are often held over a measure to join the first and third beats. Orsa ornamentation includes trills, occasional double-string chords, and quarter tones. One of the Orsa polskas taught in the workshop, "Vallåtspolskan," is transcribed at the end of this article. *Vallåt* means "herding tune," and the polska is related to songs rural girls made up to bring their cows together.

The status of fiddlers varied greatly from region to region in pre-industrial Sweden. In many parts of Dalarna, Björn's native province, the local fiddlers were honorable citizens. Many of them achieved great fame in neighboring villages as well as their own. In other regions, southern Sweden for example, fiddlers were outcasts, hired as itinerant laborers when they weren't playing for low-life dances or taverns. Many old instruments were crudely made from common materials, including wooden shoes. Fine instruments and good strings were only available to "respectable" musicians, like those who entertained the aristocracy. Archaic tunings we consider traditional, Björn believes, developed because poor fiddlers tried to make their strings last longer by not tuning them up to pitch. This also hints at why rhythm is more important than melody in old rural dances, and the bowing defines the rhythm.

Björn Ståbi was honored with the gold Zorn Medal in 1986 for his outstanding contribution to the preservation, performance, and teaching of the Orsa traditions within Swedish folk music. The "Zorn Award" is a concept unique to Sweden. It was established by Anders Zorn, a famous painter concerned with the disappearance of folk culture in the early 20th century. Zorn (who was also Björn's great uncle) envisioned the award as a way to stimulate interest in the preservation of old musical styles by new generations.

Björn and his wife Viveka host a weekend course each May called "Hövrastämma," at their home in Hälsingland. Many of the country's best fiddlers, nyckelharpists, accordionists and other musicians are instructors, but others come just to be students. Among musicians, Hövrastämma is considered one of the finest workshops in the country. To find out more about attending, you can check the Hövrastämma website at www.ljusdal.se/hovra/spelstamma, or contact Viveka Ståbi, Hörrgård 219, S-820 42 Korskrogen, Sweden. Tel: 46-651-222 74; Fax: 46-651-223 55; Email: staabi@ljusdal.se

Vallåtspolskan

"The Herding Tune." Polska in the style of Gössa Anders Andersson. Transcribed by Jack Tuttle from Björn's *Orsalåtar* CD (Giga GCD-35).

"One of the most well-known and most frequently played Orsa tunes." — Björn Ståbi

Discography

- Björn Ståbi, *Orsalåtar* (Giga Folkmusik HB GCD-35, 1997). Björn's solo CD. The 32 tunes were recorded in one sitting. Björn commented, "I could have recorded 32 more!" A beautifully produced and important recording for all fiddlers to hear.
- *Per Hans Olsson and Björn Ståbi* (Giga Folkmusik HB GCD-25, 1995). Per Hans Olsson is a third generation fiddler from the Rättvik area of Dalarna. Like Björn, he is a bridge to the old masters, but has his own unique signature style. A mix of traditional tunes from around Sweden and originals.
- *Three Swedish Fiddlers: Per Hans, Björn Ståbi, Kalle Almlöf* (Shanachie 21001). A CD reissue of a recording they made in the '70s, *Three Swedish Fiddlers* is a collection of performances.
- *Låtar från Orsa och Älvdalen/ Musicae Sveciae* (Caprice Records/Swedish Radio CD CAP 21476). Historical performances from Swedish Radio broadcasts, including Björn's mentor Gössa Anders Andersson.
- *Folk Fiddling from Sweden* (Nonesuch H-72033, LP). Now out of print, this was the LP that introduced Swedish fiddling to most folks outside of Sweden in the 1970s.

Giga Folkmusik HB, Borsheden, S-780 40 Mockfjärd, Sweden, (+46-241) 20080
Email: giga.folkmusik@giga.w.se
http://www.giga.w.se

Recordings can be ordered from these sources:

Norsk Ltd., Boulder, Colorado, (303) 442-6452; http://ares.csd.net/~sodaling/

Digelius Music, Helsinki, Finland. Tel: 358-0-666375; Email: pap@dighoe.pp.fi; http://personal.eunet.fi/pp/dighoe/scanmail.html

Rotspel/Tulegatan: Stockholm, Sweden. Tel/Fax: +46-8 16 04 04; Email: rotspel@wineasy.se
Web: http://www.wineasy.se/rotspel/

Waltz (efter Far)

Transcribed by Jack Tuttle, from Björn's *Orsalåtar* CD (Giga GCD-35).

"A tune I learnt from my father, Erik Ståbi. I thought the odd notes in the third repeat were one of the funniest things I'd ever heard. I laughed till I cried when I listened to it. Dad probably exaggerated it a bit. I must have been about four or five years old when I heard the tune for the first time." — Björn Ståbi

Alicia Svigals:
The Klezmer Fiddle Revival

By Patrice George

Alicia Svigals is the fiery fiddler in the center of the cutting-edge klezmer band the Klezmatics. With them, she appeared in the PBS television special "In the Fiddler's House," hosted by Itzhak Perlman. Her distinctive style of fiddling fuses historical study with personal passion. She has been active as a teacher, composer, arranger, and soloist. She was named "Best Klezmer Musician" at the Fifth International Klezmer Festival in Safed, Israel. Her new solo CD, Fidl, *is the first album of klezmer fiddle music to be recorded in recent times. In November 1997, this extremely busy musician found a bit of quiet time to discuss the fiddle's place in the world of klezmer today.*

Why did the fiddle in klezmer music have to be "revived"? How did the clarinet and other instruments become dominant in the klezmer ensemble?

The interesting thing about the klezmer revival and the fiddle is that the fiddle used to be the quintessential Jewish instrument, and it was the main instrument of klezmer bands for hundreds of years. It's hard to know exactly how it was used, because the sources are scarce and the old European Jewish communities were destroyed. The fiddle is a Jewish iconographic touchstone, appearing in folklore and stories. It was the most important klezmer instrument for hundreds of years. In little villages there probably was only one musician or fiddler. With two fiddlers, one would play rhythm and one would play melody. When the klezmer revival started here, the fiddle was supplanted by "hipper" instruments, associated with jazz, like trumpet and clarinet. Maybe the fiddle wasn't loud or urgent enough for bigger halls and bigger urban populations.

When did the current interest in klezmer — the "revival" — start?

In the late '70s a few groups started the revival, including Andy Statman, The Klezmorim, Kapelye and The Klezmer Conservatory Band. The Klezmatics were part of the second wave. We were the first to try to do something more than imitate the old recordings. Older groups took the old recordings and transcribed them, trying to achieve the sound that they heard. We really owed a lot to them, but were ready to do something else with the old material. We said: "This *was* our grandparents' music, but now it's *ours*." We're Jewish-Americans and this is our native musical language. We decided to integrate the music into something that made sense to us, as if it were Led Zeppelin, Philip Glass, or other music that we also identified with. We came together when each of us answered an ad in *The Village Voice* that a mysterious clarinetist put in, who then disappeared! We never heard from him again, but we've been together for twelve years now. Most klezmer bands don't have violinists, or haven't featured them prominently. The Klezmatics have featured the fiddle, partly because there are only six of us and we're a collective, so everybody is a soloist with a voice.

Interest in klezmer fiddle increased with the founding of Klezkamp. Unlike other camps which are in the summer, this is in the winter, in one of these old resort hotels in the Catskills. Around 450 people come, ranging from older folks to families. It's become the focal point for klezmer music all over the world. It offers a place both for students and the professional musicians to get together, exchange ideas, collaborate, start new projects, and start new bands. It's a community that's very close knit and wonderful.

Part of the problem with learning to play klezmer violin has been the absence of old fiddle recordings and older players to learn from. The violin didn't record well in the early days. There was one older violin player in New York, Leon Schwartz, who died a few years ago at age eighty-eight. There are more senior clarinet players, and also hundreds of old clarinet recordings.

In the '70s many fiddlers who tried to play klezmer didn't have a concept for it, so they would play in a schmaltzy gypsy style. In the old recordings you can hear that the fiddle is really imitating the old cantorial style of singing. It's a mystery until you unlock the key to exactly what to do with the violin to make those strange, sobbing sounds. I studied old recordings and worked with Leon Schwartz to figure it all out. I've fused those old fiddle techniques for Jewish music with the more virtuosic clarinet music. After developing the technique, I started playing the music associated with klezmer clarinet playing, which is much more involved than fiddle music was. Then I added a timbral concept, because you can't really hear what the tone or the timbre was like in the old music. Klezmer music is very much related to Turkish music, Greek music, Romanian music. There's a certain kind of non-western sounding timbre which is used in that kind of music, which seems very fitting for this. My sound is a combination of old fiddle style, clarinet technique, and this sort of Greek-Turkish timbre (I also play Greek fiddle). What I do is half reconstructed, half invented. This is probably true of a lot of ethnic music styles. I tend to pour on the ornamentation. I'm kind of a "baroque" player in that way. Those sounds imitate the cantor singing with a kind of wailing, very emotional tone. This music is extremely passionate, so I put that ornamented sound in the way I feel it.

"...An important thing about klezmer is that it really grew up in this country. It's an ethnic American music form in the same way that Cajun music is or the way Irish music became contradance music... It's had a hundred years to develop in this country."

...An important thing about klezmer is that it really grew up in this country. It's an ethnic American music form in the same way that Cajun music is or the way Irish music became contradance music. The whole European branch of klezmer music was killed off. It's had a hundred years to develop in this country. The clarinet as lead instrument, thought of as the klezmer tradition, really happened in this country.

Has Itzhak Perlman's public television production about klezmer music, "In the Fiddler's House," changed the audience for klezmer music, and fiddle in particular?

That's been really good...It's brought klezmer into the public eye in a way it'd never been before...Someone at Channel Thirteen (New York's PBS affiliate station) approached Perlman with the idea of exploring his musical roots. He had been thinking of it already himself, so he jumped on it. He picked four of the groups that he liked the best to work with him on the project. The television show has led to several tours with Perlman. These tours are a reunion for most of us, who started our bands when we were young. Now we tour together with our small children.

What do the Israelis think of contemporary klezmer music?

Early on in the history of Zionism there was a battle about the whole question of what should be the national language: Yiddish or Hebrew. Those on the side of Yiddish really lost out, because the language was associated with painful memories. Klezmer is Yiddish music so there's a distaste for klezmer that has gone on for many years. They still have a very ambivalent relationship to it. We played in a klezmer festival there. The crowds seemed to think of it as the music of their great-grandparents. But a new generation is coming up in Israel that doesn't have the same hang-ups. They're taking a second look at Yiddish, and klezmer music.

Here klezmer has become the music of progressive Jewish youth. It doesn't have the religious song texts which can be problematic for non-religious people. It's secular music, party music, dance music. Of course, you could say that everything Jewish is ultimately religious — even the "secular" klezmer dance tunes started out as religious melodies set to a dance beat — so it's all very intertwined. But if you want secular Jewish music, this is as close as you can get. In Israel it's a whole other thing. Klezmer has become associated with the religious contingent. That affects how the audience hears it.

What is the story of Fidl, *your new recording?*

I wanted to make a record of the klezmer fiddle music that I'd always wanted to hear, but was never available. It includes instruments generally not heard in contemporary klezmer bands, like the tsimbl (a hammered dulcimer). It's a beautiful, ethereal, magical instrument, once the most important accompaniment to the fiddle. Another neglected instrument is the wooden flute. Matt Darriau, the Klezmatics' clarinetist, played it on *Fidl,* and in the Klezmatics' score for "A Dybbuk." I also included arrangements for bowed-bass, tsimbl, wooden flute, and fiddle. That used to be a classic combination, but is seldom heard now.

Multiple fiddles are another traditionally important, beautiful sound. In a contemporary klezmer scene dominated by drums, clarinets, horns, it is a completely different, but valid, klezmer sound. I've recorded duets, trios, and quartets with three violins and a bass. On some cuts I played both melody parts, recorded and dubbed in different octaves. The other fiddler on the album, Steve Greenman, plays rhythm parts. He is a former student of mine who is now a terrific klezmer player with his own style.

Do you improvise much within a klezmer band?

Traditional klezmer improvisation is about varying the melody. It falls somewhere on the continuum between the approach of a classical musician reading the notes the same way every time, and a jazz musician who is always creating new melodies. It's a tricky thing — there is a gray area about what is still the melody, and what has gone over the edge into a new melody. The rhythm of the melody is what varies the most. Then you can vary the melody a little bit by adding or subtracting notes.

You also do a lot of arrangements, and compose original music. Do you compose on paper or keyboards, or on your fiddle?

What I've done has mainly been within the context of the Klezmatics, and for commission situations like theater, dance and film. I have music going in my head all the time, like a soundtrack to everything I do. I don't compose on the violin. When I'm walking the dog, I take a little tape recorder and sing into it along the way. The trick to composing for me is to capture a tune before it's gone.

Discography
- *Fidl,* Traditional Crossroads CD 4286, 1997 (Svigals' solo CD)
- *The Well,* The Klezmatics (with singer Chava Albersteyn), Xenophile
- *Possessed,* Xenophile 4050, 1997 (original music for Tony Kushner's play *A Dybbuk,* composed by The Klezmatics)

- *Jews With Horns,* The Klezmatics, Piranha (Germany), CD, 1994 (Order through Green Linnett/Xenophile — see below)
- *Rhythm + Jews,* Flying Fish, FF 70591, 1992 (Order through Rounder, (800) 443-4727)
- *Klezmer: A Marriage of Heaven and Earth,* Compilation, Ellipsis Arts

- *In the Fiddler's House* and *Live in the Fiddler's House,* EMI/Angel (Itzhak Perlman with contemporary klezmer ensembles.)

Traditional Crossroads: (800) 422-6282
Green Linnet/Xenophile: (800) 468-6644
Klezcamp information: (212) 691-1272

Glazier's Hora

Composed and transcribed by Alicia as played on her *Fidl* CD (Traditional Crossroads CD 4286).

Notes on the transcription: K = "krechz" — a small, harmonic-like ornament played at end of note with the 4th finger.

tr = trill — a half step. B = Bend: bend the note slightly flat and then back again, by leaning the finger back.

95

Athena Tergis and Laura Risk: Journey Begun

By Mary Larsen

Athena Tergis and Laura Risk are a young Celtic fiddling duo from San Francisco, California, playing a mix of traditional and original tunes. I had the opportunity to talk with them about their music at the 1995 North American Folk Music and Dance Alliance conference in Portland, Oregon. In addition to their musical talent, both exude a passion and enthusiasm for their music, and it's little wonder they are attracting such positive attention in the fiddling world.

Friends since pre-school, the two have been playing violin or fiddle since their early elementary school years. It all began when Laura's parents received a flier from a couple of teachers of the Suzuki method. Laura relates, "Probably one of my earliest memories is of sitting on the couch, staring out the window, and my mom coming over to me and saying, 'Hey, Laura, do you want to learn how to play the violin?' I said, 'Oh, whatever, I don't care.'" Shortly thereafter, she played at Athena's parents' wedding, sparking Athena's admiration and competitive spirit. Athena began taking lessons from the same Suzuki teacher. "And I think that's really been a blessing for us," says Athena, "because the whole theory about Suzuki is learning to play by ear, and that's really what folk music is all about. So I took about ten years of classical lessons; Laura took a bit more."

Photo: Christine Alicino

When Athena was about nine years old, she began taking lessons from Cait Reed, an Irish fiddle teacher. While Athena had felt forced to play classical music and rigid rules about practicing caused some resentment, Celtic music was like a breath of fresh air to her. One summer, her teacher was planning a trip to the Valley of the Moon Scottish Fiddling Camp, and needed a baby-sitter for her young daughter. So Athena accompanied them and fell in love with the music and the camp. After her first year there, she tied for first place in the junior category of a fiddling competition. The next year, 1987, she was named Junior National Scottish Fiddling Champion, as well as in 1988 and 1989. Athena persuaded a somewhat reluctant Laura to accompany her to the camp the second year. "I was thirteen and I was very impressionable," says Laura. "It just blew me away. Here were all these people playing music and having a really good time… I'd never heard fiddling before, really…I was hooked."

Having attended Valley of the Moon for ten years (last year as teachers), Laura and Athena credit the school with cultivating their style. From Scottish fiddlers such as Alasdair Fraser and Aly Bain to Cape Breton fiddlers like Buddy MacMaster and Jerry Holland, the school has always attracted a variety of Celtic greats. It was Alasdair Fraser who first suggested the girls do a duet for a scholarship fund-raiser — an idea that proved to be an excellent one.

The girls had other musical interests as well: Athena listened to jazz and pop and played in a rock band; Laura played with the San Francisco Symphony Youth Orchestra, and also enjoyed playing jazz and bluegrass. These various other influences began to make appearances in their traditional tunes, which was one reason they decided to begin writing their own. Laura explains, "Once you've written a tune, you really have complete freedom to do whatever you want, because nobody can tell you how it was meant to be: 'Well, that's not the traditional way to play that tune!'" Athena continues, "I think that's why we started writing our own tunes, because there's a lot of opinions on what's traditional and what's not, and we were tired of hearing it!" The composing process is a natural one for them. "Very, very rarely do we sit down with note paper and figure out harmonies," says Athena. "The only thing we use paper for is to write down the harmonies after they've been created so that we actually remember it the next time around," adds Laura. "Then we usually lose the paper, so it doesn't really do much good!"

Laura and Athena produced their album, *Journey Begun,* on Alasdair Fraser's Culburnie Records label. Described by Athena as "kind of a representation of the last seven years of our lives," the album is a mixture of traditional and original tunes. Eschewing the usual method of recording separate tracks in a studio, Laura and Athena, joined by Steve Baughman (guitar), Peter Maund (percussion), Pat Klobas (bass), and Alasdair Fraser (violin on one track), recorded the album in a church in Marin County. Laura says, "Great acoustics. We put one mic up, and we stood in a semi-circle and just played."

"You need to have music going at all points in your life if you can. Go and get a CD by some great fiddler and listen to it literally fifty times — memorize the thing..." — Laura

"When you're dreaming tunes, you know that you've listened to enough tapes." — Athena

Asked if they had any tips for aspiring fiddlers, Athena says, "Listen. Find people you like and ask them who they listen to. If I have any regrets, it's that I spent a lot of time only listening to a few things, a few people, and playing a very specific kind of thing and being really happy with that. Don't try to be perfect." Laura explains, "Athena and I both have a lot of students, and the ones who really seem to be getting it are the ones that are listening to everything. You need to have music going at all points in your life if you can. Go and get a CD by some great fiddler and listen to it literally fifty times — memorize the thing...." Athena adds, "The biggest thing in Celtic music, I think, is the rhythm. So the best thing you can do is go and vacuum your floor with your headphones on and bop around to it... When you're dreaming tunes, you know that you've listened to enough tapes."

The Journey Continues: Since this article was written in 1995, Laura and Athena have gone on to a host of new projects.

Athena Tergis:

Recording *Journey Begun* with Laura Risk was a turning point in both our lives. We realized what was possible, where music could take us, and also that we needed to explore our own directions and define what "life as a musician" meant to each of us. For me, that journey took me to Ireland in 1995, where I lived and played for three years, touring in Ireland and throughout Europe with many different line-ups and bands. From the moment I arrived, I was hooked! I was out in local pubs playing every night, listening, watching, and at first, making a lot of unpleasant noises on the fiddle! Before long I found myself in sessions with amazing musicians, one of whom was Sharon Shannon, renowned box accordion player. She asked me to join The Sharon Shannon Band for their 1997 European festival tour which included the Cambridge and Glastonbury folk festivals, the recording of the Gail Force series at the Point Depot in Dublin, and many other major festivals and concerts throughout Europe.

My current adventure is set in London. I moved here in 1998, for a change of scenery and new musical challenges. A few short months later I was invited to feature in the "Lord Of The Dance" production in Las Vegas, where I spent three months before returning to London to pursue my own musical interests. Since my return, I have played throughout London with many different artists and outfits and I have begun recording my own album which will be finished in July '99.

For me, playing the fiddle gives me a language to express what I wouldn't say in words. We all hear music differently, so by playing with others we can inspire each other in surprising ways. Traditional music by its very nature brings people together, and to me that community is the most rewarding part of playing the fiddle. When first learning to play, it's easy to be intimidated and discouraged, but seek out fellow fiddlers and I think you'll find the excitement of playing together is nearly as infectious as the tunes are themselves!

For bookings or information, contact Athena in London at (011 44) 7977 269953.

Laura Risk:

After graduating from the University of California at Berkeley with a degree in Applied Math, Laura moved to Boston to pursue music full-time. She currently plays with hammer dulcimer player Ken Kolodner and multi-instrumentalist Robin Bullock in Greenfire, a Celtic ensemble on Dorian Records. Laura's first solo recording, *Celtic Dialogue,* was released in early 1999 on Dorian Records. The album explores the fiddle music of eighteenth century Scotland in collaboration with PBS "Civil War" pianist Jacqueline Schwab. In addition, Laura is a music instructor at Wellesley College.

A member of the American roots band Cordelia's Dad from 1996-98, Laura has also performed with the John Whelan Band, Ensemble Galilei, Philharmonia Baroque Orchestra and the American Bach Soloists. She has appeared at many of North America's most prestigious acoustic music festivals, including the Newport Folk Festival, Celtic Colours (Cape Breton Island), City States (Birmingham), the Winnipeg Folk Festival and the Philadelphia Folk Festival. Recent television appearances include CFTO TV's "Eye on Toronto," WGBY's "Caught in the Act" (Springfield, MA), and WMAR's "Christmas with the Baltimore Choral Arts Society."

For bookings or other information, contact Laura at LRISK@WELLESLEY.EDU or (617) 625-5661.

Selected Discography — Laura Risk

- *Celtic Dialogue* (Dorian Records, 1999)
- *Greenfire,* with Ken Kolodner and Robin Bullock (Dorian Records, 1998)
- *Spine,* with Cordelia's Dad (Appleseed Records, 1998)
- *Host of the Air: Contemporary Music for Scottish Country Dancing* (1998)
- *Walking Stones,* with Ken Kolodner and Robin Bullock (Dorian Records, 1997)
- *Journey Begun,* with Athena Tergis (Culburnie Records, 1994)

[Culburnie Records, P.O. Box 219, Nevada City, CA 95959, (800) 830-6296/(530) 292-4219; email: usinfo@culburnie.com; website: http://www.culburnie.com.]

The New House

Jay Ungar: Infecting the World with Fiddle Fever

By Peter Anick

Photo: Michael Weisbrot

Jay Ungar and Molly Mason

Jay Ungar, well known in the folk music community through his fiddling with the David Bromberg Band, Fiddle Fever and Molly Mason, has received international recognition for his composition, "Ashokan Farewell," which served as the theme for the Grammy Award-winning soundtrack of Ken Burns' public television documentary, "The Civil War." In addition to frequent concert and radio appearances, Jay and Molly run several week-long Fiddle and Dance workshops in the Catskills each summer. It was at one of these ("Southern Week") that we held this interview, during a break between teaching classes and playing for dances, and our conversation often drifted back to the music camp that was in full swing outside the trailer's door.

How did you first react to this (folk) music when you heard it?

When I was in high school (the High School of Music and Art in New York City), I was interested in all kinds of music in a very peripheral way. I didn't get deeply into anything but classical music, which was what I had taken lessons in and was playing in high school. But there were so many other musical people that I wound up hearing more than had been available in the 1950s in the Bronx. One friend in particular had a bunch of Flatt and Scruggs and Stanley Brothers bluegrass albums. People would trade these things on reel to reel tapes in those days, because the albums were so hard to get in New York. It was in the early '60s when I really got attracted to that music. I think it was because I was a kid who grew up in New York City and didn't really like the city, and that music came from somewhere else, and it was old. I wasn't thrilled with the '50s that we had just lived through, and it harkened back to an earlier time and a simpler lifestyle and all that sort of thing. It was fun and exciting, and there was improvisation involved. Some people say that there was improvising in classical music during the Baroque period, but today there isn't much. I enjoyed the idea of people having their own take on something, yet it being a tradition. An individual approach, and self-expression, yet having some connection to the past and to something meaningful — like a rural environment, a simpler lifestyle.

Did you see the performers or did you just hear the records at that point?

At that point, I was anxious to see and hear people. The first old-time musicians I got to see were the New Lost City Ramblers. They would recreate cuts from old 78s, in a sense, live on stage. Around that time, just after I got out of high school, I went to the Newport Folk Festival. Must have been the summer of '64, I guess, or '65, and that's where I heard Bill Monroe and his band and a Cajun group with Dewey Balfa. I didn't know who he was at the time, but I remember walking across a field, hearing them in the distance — they were playing at a workshop stage — and I just couldn't believe the sound! It wasn't that I loved it or hated it — I was drawn to it magnetically. What is this? And then when I got there and I watched them singing, these sounds in another language coming out of their mouths, I was really transported by it.

A number of years later, early '70s, I was in a band called the Putnam String County Band, with John Cohen (who was in the New Lost City Ramblers), my first wife, Lyn Hardy on guitar, and Abby Newton on cello...Being one of the few performing string bands in 1970 and '71, we wound up getting a lot of work. As a result, I wound up meeting some really great players. That's around when I met Dewey Balfa, when the Balfa Brothers were traveling and we were on the same festivals. I would get to play with Dewey, you know, at jam sessions late at night. He just loved to be playing till three, four in the morning with young people who were interested. And I remember it took many years before he gave me a nod of approval. He was really a natural teacher in the sense of always being ready to tell you when you're not doing it right, but with encouragement to keep trying. I knew for sure that I didn't have it at that point, but I had his approval to keep trying and knew he thought I could get it eventually! There wasn't much said. He did that with a lot of people and mentored them that way....

Getting back to those 1960s Greenwich Village jam sessions, I'd sometimes feel a certain negative vibe if I would try to sit in. You know, people would kind of turn and their body language would say, "You're not welcome." I kept trying to figure out what the clues were, you know, what you had to do to get it right. It wasn't apparent. I felt with Dewey, you were always welcome, and he let you know what he needed for you to be welcome. I think, that's a really important thing — to help people get an entry into this. I see it as a goal of the camps

"We have to do these camps, because this is what really feeds the soul — being here. I don't think I'd give a very good concert if I hadn't been to Ashokan in the summer! I really need it."

at Ashokan. I think, in starting Ashokan, my feeling was to try to create a place where you could really be a beginner and you could learn the rules, in a safe environment where you're not going to be at risk all the time socially... It should be a comfortable place for people who are professionals and great players as well — a place where people of all levels of expertise can be together and get something from each other. I think one of the nice things about Ashokan is that somebody who's really great at one thing can be a beginner at something else. For me that concept came from a music and dance camp called "Camp Akiba" in Pennsylvania in 1978. This camp only happened once. There were about forty wonderful staffers, which included the New Lost City Ramblers and the Green Grass Cloggers, and every type of music in the folk tradition — Irish and Scottish, what have you. There were only twelve participants attending. As a result, we all took each other's classes, in order to fill the classes up, and it was great to see somebody who was an absolutely fantastic dancer be a beginning fiddler or an absolutely spectacular banjo player be a beginning dancer. It was really an eye opener, and everybody was equal in some way there. This was the inspiration for Ashokan. Most of the people who teach here are really specialists in a style, and I'm a little more of a, you know, I dabble in many styles. I haven't zeroed in on one thing and stuck with it. That's just my natural tendency. So I tend to be a little different, but I've enjoyed bringing together people who are more specialists here, to learn from, and I feel I'm learning from them. It's a great environment.

How old were you when you started composing?

I started playing the violin at seven and I immediately made up melodies of some kind. I have no idea what they were. It was just play, playfulness, which I try to keep it today. It actually surprised me at first when my tunes were valuable to other people. I would just play them at dances because I like to do it. Then I found that other people were learning them. So I think I've always enjoyed just playing around, making up music...As soon as I started playing fiddle music, I started making up fiddle tunes, when I had that kind of structure in mind. Usually an A part and a B part. Usually 32 bars, but not always. Sometimes I make up a three-part tune, or a crooked tune or what have you. When I started to notice that there were certain characteristics of the different fiddle traditions, I'd try to make up a Cape Breton tune or a New England tune, or a Cajun tune, and try to find something that crossed some of those boundaries occasionally. "Ashokan Farewell" for me, was a Scottish lament....

I remember when I heard "The Lovers' Waltz" on the radio for the first time, it really jumped out at me.

Molly and I wrote "The Lovers' Waltz" together ten years ago, and we really liked it, but thought it was more personal than anything else. And we did not really want to play it for other people, because when something means a lot to you, and you play it for someone else and they are totally unaffected by it... [laughs] you kind of feel bad, you know, deflated by that experience? So we really didn't play it for anybody for awhile. Then we played it with Russ Barenberg the guitarist, just kind of tentatively threw it in while we were sitting around in the living room playing some tunes. He said, "Oh, that's a really luxurious tune. You can really lay back, like in a thick couch!" That was pretty encouraging. Then, we played it here at Ashokan, at a late night jam session where people were playing waltz after waltz. And it struck folks nicely, and we started playing it at dances. It eventually grew into our concert repertoire and we recorded it. It's now one of our most requested tunes.

You seem to do a lot of things around here that are beyond the music, in terms of community building.

Yeah, that's become really important to Molly and me...I think most of it is the idea of consensus and trying to not have too many rules. Basically, we believe that people will do really great things if they have the room to do them, and encouragement. That's the bottom line of what we try to do here at Ashokan. Some years it's just nice and pleasant and other years it's amazing, some of the things that happen. You just can't predict it.... One of the beautiful things about camps like this is that you're exposed twenty-four hours a day to people emoting through music and dance, and it just brings you alive. You can go to no classes and still come away a better player. You lie down to go to sleep and there's gonna be somebody still playing music! It's going into your psyche there as you're sleeping! It's gratifying that in the past five years, Molly and I have had a lot more offers to do concerts. We really enjoy doing them and it's a great opportunity. We began to think, "How can we keep running these camps and doing all of these concerts?" We had to really think about that... But we have to do these camps, because this is what really feeds the soul — being here. I don't think I'd give a very good concert if I hadn't been to Ashokan in the summer! I really need it.

[For information on recordings, please call 1-800-40-MUSIC. For information on bookings, recordings, Ashokan Fiddle & Dance or Swinging Door Music, contact Jay and Molly at 987 Rt. 28A, West Hurley, NY 12491; (800) 292-0905/(914) 338-2996; ashokan@aol.com; website: http://www.jayandmolly.com.

Angel Records, 304 Park Ave. South, New York, NY 10010; (212) 253-3000; http://www.angelrecords.com

The Lovers' Waltz

By Jay Ungar and Molly Mason. ©1993 by Swinging Door Music–BMI. Used by permission.
All rights reserved. From the album *The Lovers' Waltz* (Angel Records 7243 5 55561).

Québec Fiddler Extraordinaire
Jean-Marie Verret

By Guy Bouchard
(Translated by Laura Sadowsky)

Jean-Marie Verret grew up in a very musically rich family and for many, he is the most authentic of all today's Québécois fiddlers. His father, Jules Verret (1916-1982), was one of the most prestigious fiddlers of his time. Near the end of his career (1974), he made a recording with Philo (PH 2007). The Verrets are not only virtuoso instrumentalists but they also inherited a unique repertoire from the 19th-century French quadrille style. Jean-Marie's musical career is highly varied and he is one of our best known fiddlers. With a flamboyant virtuoso style, he is an expert dance musician, leaving no one indifferent to his music. He is perhaps the last of the Québécois fiddlers who learned his style and repertoire in a purely traditional fashion.

Jean-Marie, where were you born?

I was born on February 9, 1945, in Lac St-Charles, a little town about fifteen miles north of Québec City where I still live today. I am the fifth child in a family of thirteen children!

Your family is one of the most well-known families in Québec traditional music. Tell us about the main musicians.

My first influence and my idol has always been my father Jules, who was a truly exceptional fiddler. He learned his music from a man named Pit Jornoch [a nickname for Pierre Verret, 1863-1937] who lived in the neighboring parish. My father always considered him to be the greatest fiddler he had ever heard in his life. I was told that Pierre Verret learned his repertoire and style from Charlot Parent from Charlesbourg, which is a few kilometers southeast, and at the time was just a village. My father often played with his brothers Roméo and Yves. Roméo was also the best step dancer in the family, whereas Yves was an extraordinary accordion player. My grandfather Jean-Baptiste also played accordion and all the *veillées* (get-togethers or house parties) took place there. All the musicians from the area, including the Verrets from Stoneham as well as all the most famous traditional musicians from Québec such as Théodore Dugauy and Jos Bouchard stopped by my grandfather's at one time or another. Later, these *veillées* were at my father's house. My grandfather was accompanied on the piano by my aunt Jacqueline. Today, I often play with my brother Yvan on accordion and my sister Lise on piano. Lise, the youngest of the family, also backed up my father.

So, you started playing at a young age. How did that come about?

I have always been fascinated with the fiddle, and even though I heard my uncle Yves, an accordion virtuoso, I have always only loved the fiddle. I started playing at the age of 10. We did not have a 3/4 or 1/2 size fiddle so I had trouble playing on a standard size fiddle. My father didn't really help me until I was about 14. But already at age 11, I played my first gig with John Ness on the piano-accordion and Charlie Morin on banjo. I was paid $2.00 for the night and the *soirée* ended at 3 a.m. We played quadrilles, polkas, waltzes, brandys and caledonias. If my father heard me playing one of his tunes incorrectly, he would tell me to stop playing it and that he would show me how to play it right afterwards.

Were you already aware at that time that your family repertoire was unique?

Yes. I had heard Don Messer on TV, and we had all the 78s of Joseph Allard, Isidore Soucy, Jos Bouchard, Théodore Duguay, Fortunat Malouin and Willie Ringuette. It was obvious to me that they weren't playing the same thing as we were. The same goes for the dancing: square sets were unusual in the Québec City area and it seemed to us that the music for these dances was played much too fast! Therefore, I realized very early on that our family had a specific heritage. When I was around 16, I bought a tape machine and began to record my father's tunes. He didn't like the tape machine very much that I stuck on the floor, but his repertoire was so vast that I couldn't conceive of how I could remember it all. He could play for weeks on end and I would never hear the same tune twice!

They always played for dances. Were there specific tunes for each part of the dance?

My father and my uncle played all over the area for dances. They played for quadrilles, brandys and caledonias. They had an incredible

> *"[My father's] repertoire was so vast that I couldn't conceive of how I could remember it all. He could play for weeks on end and I would never hear the same tune twice!"*

knowledge of which tunes to play for each part of the dance. It was absolutely out of the question to play the second part of a caledonia for the third part of a quadrille. They also knew how each little village wanted the tunes played so that later on, when I was hired to play for these dances, they gave me advice on which tunes to play. They would tell me, if you are going to play at that village for that family, play this particular tune for the fourth part — they love that one!

Have you kept this knowledge?

Absolutely. I know very well and practically by instinct which tunes to play for which dances. I also realize that not only do very few musicians today have this knowledge, but also that the dancers themselves and often the callers are not aware of this. I have to say that the dances in my area were never called. Everyone just knew them.

Who were your other influences?

Other than my father, the only other player who really influenced me was Jos Bouchard. He knew my father very well because he had played many times with him at my grandfather Jean-Baptiste's house. Jos Bouchard had become very well known because of the numerous 78s he recorded and the radio shows he did with groups like *Les Montagnards laurentiens.* My father had always refused to make a career of music, and he also refused offers to play on the radio or on records. With thirteen children at home, he couldn't miss one day of work. I met Jos Bouchard on the Island of Orleans where I was working as a butcher at the time. When I saw him come in, I told him that he knew my father well. When he realized I was Jules' son, he invited me to his house. That was around 1973. I loved his style, and every day for five years during my lunch hour I went over to his place. After that, I was able to play exactly like him. His ornamentation and bowing were not like my father's but he had a unique way of playing and bringing out melodies.

Did you ever meet Jean Carignan?

Yes, and I remember very well the first time he came to our house. I was playing regularly with Jos Bouchard, who introduced me to Philippe Bruneau who had been playing with Carignan for a long time. One day, I invited Philippe and Jean to come and meet my father. When I got home, I told my father that we were going to have company. When he found out who I had invited, he got really mad. He had just finished a really rough day at work and he was in no mood to play his fiddle. Finally, he realized that it was too late to change anything, so he invited my Uncle Yves over and got ready for these special guests. I wish you could have seen the expression on Philippe's face when he heard my Uncle Yves play the accordion. And then when Jules started playing the fiddle, Philippe kept saying to Ti-Jean [a nickname meaning "little Jean"]: "See, I told you there was such a thing as Québécois music." You have to understand that there was a never-ending discussion between those two about folk music. Jean thought that Québécois folk music was simply Irish music played badly whereas Philippe recognized the existence of an authentic Québec music having a particular accent and a specific repertoire. They played all night, and it was one of the rare occasions that my father didn't go to work the next day. They all had great admiration for one another.

We have often heard you in concert or at dances playing with an accordion. Is this an instrument you enjoy playing with?

Yes and no — I have always played with accordions and the greatest players, starting with my uncle Yves. I am used to playing with an accordion so that today, it doesn't bother me at all. But I prefer playing with fiddlers. Button accordions are limited so we often have to change the key of the tune so that we can play it together. Many tunes just can't be played on the accordion. Today, I am very happy and proud to play with my son Martin. Unlike myself, who can't read a single note of music, Martin (age eighteen) is being classically trained while continuing to learn fiddling techniques. He played with me on my last two recordings.

Even though it was not always indicated on your record jackets, some of your own compositions are on your records. Which ones are these exactly?

I have composed tunes in the style of my family repertoire and I sometimes didn't specify it, such as "La Gigue du lac," which is on my first recording with Philo. However, on the latest CD, I composed "Le Reel de St-Aimé des lacs" and "Fantaisie de l'an 2000," a waltz to go with "Le Valse des roses des frères Pigeon." At that time, I hadn't realized the importance of specifying this information, but I know now that it is essential to give as much information as possible about the tunes we record.

Do you make your living only from music?

Not at all. I work for the provincial transportation department and in the summertime, I run a snack bar.

Are you satisfied with your latest recording Quadrilles du XIXe et XXe siècles?

Very much so. This is my first recording on CD and I think that it is by far the best recording. I have continued to concentrate on my family repertoire and I am pleased that it can be shared in this way. Lise, Martin and I played all the tunes together without any dubbing. It is a live studio recording. We wanted to capture the magical feeling of a live recording. Only Luc Lavallée's guitar was added.

Tell us a little about your career and your upcoming projects.

I have played with just about everyone in Québec, and I have also travelled a lot both in Europe and the United States. I have often played with accordion player Philippe Bruneau and more recently with Raynald Ouellet. I have given concerts, workshops, played on TV and at major festivals, and I am on my fifth recording. I would really like to do a tribute to Jos Bouchard, and there's a good possibility that this will be my next CD. I would also like to do a recording with my brother Yvan on accordion. As for the Verret family repertoire, I should be able to record many more CDs before running out of tunes and that is only using the most interesting ones! I hope to continue making recordings with my family, Martin and Lise. In addition to playing for dances, I hope to continue participating in music and dance camps such as Ashokan and maybe bringing Martin along to share with everyone the sound of our two fiddles.

Discography

- *Quadrilles du XIXe et XXe siècles* (Thirty Below TB-134-CD / TB-135-CAS) 1997
- *Reflets du passé* (Thirty Below TB-054-CAS) 1993
- *Hommage à Pit Jornoch* (Thirty Below TB-053-CAS) 1984

- *Jules Verret* (Philo 2007) 1974 (No longer available)
- *Jean-Marie Verret* (Philo 42016) 1975 (No longer available)
- *The French Canadian Dance Music* (Folkways RF 120) 1980 (No longer available)

Jean-Marie Verret's three most recent recordings can be ordered by contacting:
Trente Sous Zéro / Thirty Below: 1108, rue Dollard, Val-Bélair, Québec, Canada G3K 1W6. Telephone & fax: (418) 847-9815.
Email: thirtybe@qbc.clic.net
Web: http://www.qbc.clic.net/~thirtybe

La Cadence à Ti-Jules

Transcribed by Laurie Hart and Guy Bouchard as played by Jean-Marie Verret on his *Quadrilles du XIXe et XXe siècles* album.
"Ti-Jules" refers to Jean-Marie's father, Jules Verret ("Ti" is a nickname, short for "petit," meaning little or small).

Claude "Fiddler" Williams: Kansas City Swing!

By Mary Larsen

Photo: Wojtek Kubik ©1998

Claude Williams at his 90th birthday party in New York, February 23, 1998.

Kansas City Swing fiddler Claude Williams was born in Muskogee, Oklahoma, in 1908. A gifted musician at a very early age, he was playing guitar, mandolin, banjo and cello by the time he was ten. But when he heard Joe Venuti play, he knew he had to add the violin to his accomplishments. His family bought him his first violin the day after the Venuti concert, and before Williams went to bed that night, he was already playing tunes on it. Playing with his brother-in-law Ben Johnson's string band earned Williams six to seven dollars a night in tip money at a time when most people were making five or six dollars a week.

In 1928 Williams moved to Kansas City, which was fast becoming the swing capital of the country. He played guitar and violin with the Twelve Clouds of Joy and with them made his first recordings. They often played "jitney" dances, or ten-cents-a-dance dances, which necessitated a large number of short tunes (or parts of longer ones). He frequently jammed with other great jazz and swing players such as Charlie Parker, Lester Young, and Mary Lou Williams. He learned to play his fiddle loud to compete with reed and brass instruments. In the mid 1930s, Williams joined up with Count Basie as his guitarist. When he was replaced in the Basie Orchestra by guitarist Freddie Green, Williams went on to lead a variety of bands. In 1980, Classic Jazz released *Fiddler's Dream,* the last recording to feature Williams' guitar soloing. Since then he has stayed with the violin.

During the 1980s, Claude played in the Paris production of Black and Blue, followed by an award-winning run in New York with Roland Hanna and Grady Tate. He was the first inductee into the Oklahoma Jazz Hall of Fame. Since 1990 he's been featured on "CBS News Sunday Morning," and has played both Carnegie and Lincoln Center several times. Claude performed for Clinton's first inaugural, toured Australia and released two CDs titled *Claude Williams, Live at J's, Volumes 1 & 2,* placing on "Best of 1994" jazz critics' polls, *The Village Voice* and *Pulse!* 1994 was the first year of Mark O'Connor's fiddle camp, where Claude has participated annually since.

Black Liberated Arts, Inc. presented Williams with their first Charlie Christian Jazz Award. In the mid 1990s, NPR's "Jazz Set" featured him and he toured headlining a Masters of the Folk Violin tour. During 1995, he performed in Europe and at the JVC Jazz Festival in New York, where he returned in 1996. Claude's *SwingTime in New York* CD with Roland Hanna, Earl May and Bill Easley garnered great reviews in 1995. The Smithsonian documented him for its Jazz Oral History Project. A *Statesmen of Jazz* recording includes Claude, Milt Hinton, Al Grey, Clark Terry, Buddy Tate, Benny Waters, Panama Francis and Joe Wilder. He toured the U.S. and Japan as a Statesman.

"Fiddler" began 1997 in Europe. On his 89th birthday he educated students at the Smithsonian. Shortly thereafter, he was inducted into the Oklahoma Music Hall of fame, along with Patti Page, Woody Guthrie and Merle Haggard. Other highlights of the year included performing at Dick Hyman's "Jazz in July" in New York, opening the Greater Hartford Jazz Fest, touring Japan, a broadcast of a one-hour "Jazz Profiles – Tribute to Claude Williams" on NPR, and releasing *King of Kansas City.*

Claude's 90th birthday was a normal one for him — he played five shows in five days in four cities! On his birthday, he was honored and played in a "Strung Together" concert in Northampton, Massachusetts, with five other fiddlers with age differences spanning 74 years. Claude played the White House March 9 with Bucky Pizzarelli and Keter Betts, backing dancers Savion Glover and Jimmy Slyde for an "In Performance at the White House" PBS special, aired nationally September 16, 1998. He returned to the White House October 6 to receive the National Heritage Fellowship, awarded to him personally by Hillary Clinton.

As "Fiddler" turned 91 on February 22, 1999, he was setting plans for a concert with Johnny Gimble, Mark O'Connor, Vassar Clements and others, more teaching, at least one European tour, and his next recording. Blues will be the theme for that Rounder CD, to be recorded in New York with his favorite guitarist, Joe Cohn, pianist Henry Butler, bassist Keter Betts, drummer Jimmy Lovelace and special guest vocalist Teri Thornton. He has bookings into the next century.

How did you learn fiddle — did you take lessons?

Well, I first learned it by ear. When I got the fiddle, I had played guitar, banjo, mandolin — I had played all of those by ear. When I heard Joe Venuti, the last thing I had played was the cello. And we had taken the strings off the cello and put bass strings on it because my brother-in-law had a string band and we needed a bass player. We didn't realize the cello was also a lead instrument. When I heard Joe Venuti with a big band — I was standing about a half a block from the place — and the violin was so beautiful up over the whole band...

(Text continued on page 108.)

Back Home In Indiana

Transcribed by Jack Tuttle as played by Claude Williams on his *Live at J's, Volume 2* CD (Arhoolie 406).

Back Home In Indiana (Solo)

*"Everybody says the older I get, the better I sound, so I want to thank them for that.
Because I hope I don't just quit or retire or something before I go down the other way!"*

I told my mother, "*That's* what *I* want to play." So the next thing we did, we took the cello down and traded it for a fiddle. When I brought the fiddle home, I could play it because I'd been playing mandolin. It's the same thing — I just had to figure out how to bow the fiddle. My brother-in-law told my mother I needed to know something about music then. My first violin teacher — I could play better than he could, but I didn't know what I was doing. I learned some bowing, and I went from him to another teacher, who was really good. The first cat was a colored man, the next one was a white cat. If I'd stayed with him I'd be able to play with any symphony by now. But after I learned how to read the piano score, I thought I knew all I needed to know about the fiddle. I'd get a song down and teach it to my brother-in-law. I was learning string band stuff, popular stuff, like [sings] "How you gonna keep 'em down on the farm after they've seen Paree?"

Have you been influenced by other styles of music?

Being from Muskogee, I was over in Tulsa quite a bit playing — you know, Bob Wills and his Texas Playboys. But I never did play any of that style. I stuck to the regular jazz. Well, we called it swing then... The jazz style that I play I always likened to a tenor sax and trumpet. Louis Armstrong was the first one I heard play a diminished chord on the trumpet. I had never heard anything like that before and I got interested in the trumpet sound and the tenor sax. Ben Webster was one of my idols, and so was Louis Armstrong.

When you first went to Kansas City in 1928, did you find it difficult to break into the music scene there?

No. I came up here with the Twelve Clouds of Joy, and when we got here we were about the best band in Kansas City. We had Benny Moten's band to run up against, and George E. Lee had a big band. They were the two best bands in Kansas City. We had to rearrange a lot of our music because we had been playing for jitney dances. We never did play a song over two and a half or three minutes. So all our songs were real short and we had to add to them. But we didn't have too much trouble doing that.

Has your music changed at all as you've gotten older?

Well it might have changed a little — there's a different way you attack the notes. Everybody says the older I get, the better I sound, so I want to thank them for that. Because I hope I don't just quit or retire or something before I go down the other way!

What's your favorite environment to play in?

Mostly in nightclubs. Jam sessions at some night clubs. I always play in pretty stylish clubs, and if we have a jam session, ain't nobody gonna come up to jam unless they can play pretty good. So I enjoy it.

Do you still improvise as much as you might have at one time, or do you have the tunes pretty much worked out now?

I probably improvise now a little more. You get the right notes in a chord and you change them around, from seventh to ninth... When Duke Ellington first started playing all flat ninths and all those chords, it was over the average person's head. They were saying Duke was playing dischords, but they didn't know what they were listening to.

Do you have any advice or tips for other fiddlers?

Every time you pick up your fiddle you can learn a little bit more about it. Just practice and keep it up. That's about all you can do. You can take lessons on the fiddle for ten, fifteen years, and that's what you have to do in order to play with a good symphony, if you want to consider playing anywhere around first chair.

[Thanks to Russ Dantzler for his help with this article.]

Selected Discography
- *Upcoming CD* with a blues theme; Claude Williams with Henry Butler, Keter Betts, Joe Cohn & Teri Thornton. Rounder CD, fall '99.
- *Claude Williams: King of Kansas City,* with Rod Fleeman, Bob Bowman, Todd Strait, Karrin Allyson, Lisa Henry & Kim Park, 1997, Progressive CD 7100.
- *SwingTime in New York,* Williams with Sir Roland Hanna, Bill Easley, Earl May, and Joe Ascione, 1995, Progressive CD 7093.

- *Claude Williams Live at J's, Volume 1,* 1993, Arhoolie CD 405
- *Claude Williams Live at J's, Volume 2,* 1993, Arhoolie CD 406
- *Fiddler's Dream,* 1980, Classic Jazz LP 135; 1998 re-issued as *The Definitive Black & Blue Sessions, Claude Williams, My Silent Love,* Black & Blue CD 901.8.
- *Call for The Fiddler,* Claude Williams Quintet, 1976, SCS-1051 LP; 1994 re-issued as SteepleChase CD 31051.

- *Man From Muskogee,* Jay McShann and Claude Williams, 1972; 1995 re-issued as Sackville CD 3005.

Claude Williams' Progressive, Arhoolie and Rounder (when available) CDs may be ordered from Russ Dantzler, Hot Jazz Mgmt. & Production, 328 West 43rd St., Suite 4FW, New York, NY 10036, 212-586-8125; hotjazz@idt.net; http://soho.ios.com/~hotjazz/HOTJAZZ.html. Also contact Russ Dantzler for booking info.

George Wilson: Northern Fiddler

By Susan Conger

Even from outside the dance hall, through the open windows the fiddle has a snap and drive to it that makes you hurry inside to see who's behind that bow arm. Up on stage, above the flurry of tapping feet, you see a lanky form, a quick grin and an utterly relentless right arm: George Wilson. George, a self-described "Northern fiddler," has been playing for dances and concerts in the Northeast for over twenty years. He's coaxed everything from original melodies to Chinese tunes from his fiddle, but his special love is the music of Cape Breton.

George plays with a number of different bands, including Fennig's Allstar Stringband (with whom he has played since 1975), The Whippersnappers (which he characterizes as more of a concert band than a dance band), Taconic Tonic (playing Cape Breton and Balkan music), and Kitchen Ceili (playing Irish music). He's also played for Vanaver Caravan, a performing dance troupe that's stretched his playing into higher positions and even more eclectic music.

How did you get started on the fiddle, and when?

Well, let's see… I was in a rock and roll band in college and I mentioned to somebody that I had an old fiddle up in the attic. My older half-sister had given me one lesson on the violin when I was nine — so I am classically trained! [laughs]…I guess I wasn't that interested. So anyway, I was in this rock and roll band and mentioned about the fiddle up in the attic, and one of the guys in the band said, "Hey, you ought to try playing it," and I was young and impressionable and I said, "Yeah, I guess I should." So I got it out and strung it up the best I could. I tried playing rock and roll on it, with mixed results… I knew there was an old guy down the road from where I was living that had played fiddle in the 1930s. So I thought, "Okay, there's such a thing as northern fiddle style." I knew the popular thing was southern fiddle. Any fiddle music that I ever heard from anyone else was southern style. But I said, "Well, I'm not a Southerner, so I'm going to find out what northern fiddle music is and play that."

And this guy who played northern fiddle…

Oh, so I ended up going down to see him, but he was in his eighties and he shook so bad he couldn't play anymore. I tried to figure it out. I had just started going to contradances…and then I got a Jean Carignan record. That kind of set the course pretty well there…I started trying to imitate that, pretty poorly, but trying anyway. I puttered around with that for awhile, and then I met Allan Block, who played up at the North Bennington (Vermont) contradances. I ended up starting to play guitar for him. That was a good apprenticeship, playing guitar for a real fiddle player. He and I went to Europe a couple of times, in the fall of 1973 and 1974. So I got a lot of influence there.

When I got back from one of those trips, I was pawing through a record bin in a W.T. Grant store, and there was a bunch of fiddle records that I didn't know anything about. There were a couple of records of Graham Townsend, and I had no idea who he was, and then there were a couple of records of [Winston] Scotty Fitzgerald, and I had no idea who *he* was. But the Scotty Fitzgerald record had a lot more tunes on it, so I figured "I might as well get the one with the most tunes on it," which was a real good choice. I listened to it, and it was kind of strange at first, but I kept listening to it, and the more I listened, the more I loved it, Cape Breton fiddling. So I got hooked on that.

That was how that whole Cape Breton connection started?

Yeah, that's how it got started. Well, that same store ended up having most of the Scotty Fitzgerald albums. I got all of those, and I still have 'em. He was my hero; still is — one of them. Somewhere along the line I got some Louis Beaudoin records; I learned a bunch of those tunes, so he was another of my heroes.

Then a turning point came in my fiddle style. I'd *heard* this Scotty Fitzgerald stuff, and Jean Carignan, but I couldn't really imagine how to *do* it because I hadn't seen any of them play. But then I ended up playing bass on the *New England Chestnuts* records, in about 1980, with Rodney Miller and all those people. Watching Rod play, the swing that he put into his playing, that was really influential. Watching somebody at the same time as hearing them helps a lot. So I think I play more like Rodney Miller did back then, than he does now. Joe Cormier was another influence. He has such a nice bounce to his playing.

*"The notes, the music, is like a road map, and hearing someone play
it is like driving down the road watching the scenery."*

I've never seen anybody play waltzes the way that you play them. It's almost ferocious!

[Laughs] I play everything ferociously! It's still the rock and roll mentality. I've always played ferociously — that's as good a word as any, I guess — or intensely, maybe — that's a more positive-sounding word. I just love playing. I love playing the fiddle. Sometimes it feels like I should have a warning label on me that says, "Warning! Contents: Music under pressure."

You do some teaching — do you have any tips for fiddlers who are learning?

Well, when they're not getting a good sound, I've taken to having people try bowing with just their thumb and index finger. In order to control the bow at all, you have to push it into the string, and you get a lot cleaner sound that way. I've tried for a long time explaining it in other ways, but that all of a sudden consolidated the whole thing…I got inspired to try that by a picture in Jerry Holland's tune book, of him sitting there playing just like that; his other fingers are up in the air, he's just holding the bow with the thumb and index finger. I thought, "Hmm, he's a very clean-sounding player." When you're holding the bow like that you can't play down at the frog very well, but at the tip and in the middle you can do pretty well. The way I play I attack the notes — I try to get a good crisp attack at the beginning of the note. Trying that [bow hold], you can't get any other kind of sound; it's a crisp attack at the beginning of each note.

One piece of advice I tell people about bowing…when you're watching someone good play, the bow is doing this stuff and the hand is kind of following along for the ride. So it's the bow doing the motions, and your hand figures out how to do it somehow. So I say, don't think too much about the mechanics of what you're doing with your hand to make the bow do that. But visualize what you want the bow to do. Or what you want it to sound like. I don't know, I've never really had lessons, so this is the way I've learned things — watching people. Listening and watching both, those are big ways that I learn things.

How about left hand ideas?

Listen to yourself carefully. I kind of figured out a way to teach myself to play in tune, by using double stops. Start off with a double stop that involves an open string — put your first finger down and make sure it's exactly a fourth below the open string above it, or your third finger exactly an octave above the string below. Then build on from there. Leave that finger down in just exactly the right place, then add another one and play *that* double stop. As many doublestops as you can think of, and listen to it microscopically to make sure they're really, really, in tune. The doublestops are just like a real cross-check.

I try to remember to tell people when they're using their electronic tuner, listen real closely to what it sounds like when you're doing it. Don't just go by the lights, listen carefully and memorize what the intervals sound like. Otherwise you're not learning anything and you're becoming hooked on the tuner.

Do you play differently when you're playing for dances than with a concert group?

Sometimes I do, because I play different tunes. I don't play all that many of the same dance tunes for concerts. For dances, I experiment, I'm not as careful — which is fun. When I'm in a concert, I have to sometimes remind myself to be a little more careful because I can end up out on a limb [laughs].

I guess my philosophy about improvising on dance tunes, like jigs and reels…some people kind of like to change them into swing tunes, you know you get that impression hearing some of the modern dance players? Sometimes I guess I get fooling around and do a melodic improvisation, sort of tongue in cheek. I don't do it seriously, because I really don't believe in it. You can kind of improvise on the rhythm, on where you accent and ornament tunes, and maybe tiny little melodic changes, it can be a little different each time. But it's got to be recognizable as the same tune. I want to keep it so it's obviously the tune it was intended to be. I notice the Cape Breton players, each different one you hear playing the same tune will have their own little signature on it, they'll have two or three notes that they play differently than somebody else. I think little things like that are okay, but those old jigs and reels I think are kind of like sacred ground and I don't like to mess with them much melodically. So I have a rather conservative approach to playing.

Do you have any fiddle goals or dreams that you're pointed towards at the moment?

Well, yeah, to play as fluently and as well as possible. I've been working on higher positions. I've never done a whole lot above first position. My goals are to be less rough around the edges, to be more polished. But not less energetic. I think the ferociousness, or whatever you'd like to call it, that I play with is important.

I certainly think of it as one of your trademarks.

That's what I hear from other people, that's what I hear that people like about my playing. Playing with soul, that's a big thing. Putting your soul into it. It's important.

I guess I should give you some sage advice. It's very simple. People ask what they should do to learn how to play the fiddle. Just listen, and listen, and listen. Listen to as much fiddle music as you can and find out what you like. That's what I try to remember to tell students. You can't learn it from paper. The notes, the music is like a road map, and hearing someone play it is like driving down the road watching the scenery.

Discography

- George Wilson, *Northern Melodies,* 1995
  Fennig's All Star String Band (George
  Wilson, Bill Spence, Toby Stover):
- *The Hammered Dulcimer Returns,* Front Hall,
  FHR 041, 1992
- *Fennigmania,* Front Hall, FHR-024, 1981
- *The Hammered Dulcimer Strikes Again,* Front
  Hall, FHR-010, 1977

- *New England Chestnuts 2,* Alcazar FR 204,
  1981
- *New England Chestnuts,* Alcazar FR 203,
  1980
  (Rodney & Randy Miller; George Wilson
  plays mostly bass, but some fiddle and banjo)
- The Whipper Snappers, *Gettin' Happy,* 1988
  (George Wilson, Peter Davis, Frank Orsini)

- George Wilson & Selma Kaplan, *Off With the
  Good Saint Nicholas Boat,* 1985
- Ebenezer, *Tell It To Me,* Biograph RC-6007,
  1976 (Allan Block, George Wilson, Nancy
  McDowell)

*For lessons, bookings, or information about his
recordings, contact George Wilson at 10 Loomis
Road, Wynantskill, NY 12198, (518) 283-4957.*

Forever Young Waltz

Composed by George Wilson for the 90th birthday of Alice Davidson, ©1996. To be included on George's next album.

"This piece was commissioned by Alice Davidson's niece, Joan Ferguson, a fiddle student who is a joy to work with." — George Wilson

Jennifer and Hazel Wrigley:
Orkney's Musical Ambassadors

By Mary Larsen

Photo: Norman Chalmers

Jennifer and Hazel Wrigley of Orkney, Scotland, have been performing together throughout Europe — at dozens of festivals, folk clubs, and radio broadcasts — for over ten years. And since Jennifer won the prestigious BBC Young Tradition Award in 1997, the twins have been attracting attention and praise from an even larger audience. This interview took place before a concert in California, in February, 1997, one stop on a tour that included Hong Kong, Singapore, Bali, Australia, New Zealand, and Canada. With Jennifer's expressive fiddling and Hazel's jazzy guitar, and plenty of amusing stories about the tunes and their homeland, they put on quite a show. In addition to performing as a duo, both play with the six-piece band Seelyhoo, with Jennifer on fiddle and Hazel on guitar and piano. In order to be closer to most of their gigs ("like California!"), they're now living on the mainland of Scotland, in Edinburgh, where they're enjoying the thriving music scene. As Jennifer says, "You could probably go to a session every night of the week, and they'd all be really good."

Do you come from a musical family?

Jennifer: Not particularly. We've got a big sister who's a music teacher in Orkney. She was playing a long time before she went off to study to become a music teacher. Dad used to play piano a little bit when he was younger, but they had to get rid of the piano because it was too big for the house, so he stopped. But we always had music playing in the house; Dad loved to listen to music — all sorts of music, not just traditional stuff.

How old were you when you started playing fiddle?

Jennifer: Eight. You could get it at school when you were eight years old, so that's when I started.

How about you, Hazel, with the guitar?

Hazel: I started the guitar when I was eight as well. We went to a really small school, so you could only learn instruments that were offered to you. With the fiddle, there was a teacher employed by the local county, who was paid to come in once or twice a week. But with the guitar, it was just the normal music teacher — the one who came in to teach singing, and reading music and things. She could play the guitar, so I had guitar lessons. She only stayed for two years, so I got guitar lessons for two years, and then we got a new music teacher who couldn't play guitar, so I didn't get any more lessons. So I started teaching myself.

Have you always performed together?

Jennifer: Pretty much. Initially it started with me and my big sister Emma. We played together for a long time. We started getting asked to do things at local concerts, that kind of thing. And then Hazel started playing, too, so we've always played... I probably went on the stage first when I was about ten or something like that. I think that was the Orkney Folk Festival. I got asked to play at it because at the Orkney Folk Festival they have local concerts in some of the areas, and Deerness — that's where we're from in Orkney — they had one of these local concerts that year in the folk festival, and the sort of star fiddler they were going to have was our brother's best friend, and he fell over on the beach — he had his hands in his pockets and he broke his arm, so he couldn't play. So they said, "Oh, we'll have to get somebody else!" And we did it. That was me and my sister Emma. But when she went off to music college in Aberdeen, which is quite far away, then Hazel started playing a lot more; she got more interested in it, and we started playing together....

What is the music scene like in the Orkney Islands — are there a lot of musicians there?

Jennifer: There are a lot of musicians in Orkney. It has a very strong, rich tradition of playing... [When I was learning, my teacher told me about] the Orkney Strathspey and Reel Society, which is a group of fiddlers and accordion players who get together every Thursday night in the town hall, and play tunes. So we went, and from that, we met people that played tunes, mostly old men who had brilliant characters, and that was their only night out, Thursday night, for the Strathspey and Reel, and we all did concerts and had great fun, and loads of tunes were played.

"...The old men were all dying to know how to read music, and I was wanting to play like them, without the music!" — Jennifer

Hazel: There were all sorts of different people there — builders who were fiddle players, and joiners, and carpet layers — and you'd just meet loads of people. And each person had slightly different interests. You might meet a fiddle player who went to the Strathspey and Reel, but who really liked jazz, and therefore you met all the jazz musicians in Orkney if you knew him. So it just kind of opened the whole scene up, because it was all ages and all walks of life. There are eighteen thousand people there, so you have to know where to look. There's no specific place to go, just to meet the musicians or to hear them.

Jennifer: The Strathspey and Reel used to get invited to do concerts and things — that's how you would get out and about, and get used to playing at concerts, and from that maybe you would go to some of the outer islands. There are seventy-odd islands in Orkney, so you'd visit some outer islands with the Strathspey and Reel, at a concert, or a ceilidh. Then you would meet so many more people from that trip, and you'd just go on and on like that.

Who were some of your favorite fiddlers?

Jennifer: There was a lovely guy from Orkney called Pat Shearer. He's not with us anymore, but he was Orcadian and he played the fiddle. He got very ill when he was a bit younger, and he ended up spending a big amount of time in hospital, and that's when he started to really get going on the fiddle, and he played all the time — he was bored out of his skull, probably...He was just a real hoot. He was one of these guys at the Strathspey and Reel who would tell jokes all night. And he was a fantastic fiddle player. I really liked his playing. And then of course, there's folk from Shetland — I knew a lot of people from Shetland. The tradition in Shetland really stood a lot better chance than it did in Orkney, if you know what I mean. Because Shetland had Tom Anderson, who was teaching people left, right and center. Not just fiddle — he was teaching them the styles, how to play, but he was also teaching them the heritage of their tunes, and their culture and everything like that. Although Orkney didn't have a Tom Anderson, we all looked to Tom Anderson as an inspiration. And of course, there's all the other fiddle players as well — Sean McGuire [from Ireland], Willie Hunter from Shetland...

Hazel: And of course we used to listen to the radio... For the last fifty or sixty odd years people would listen to the radio for inspiration, so they were getting American fiddle styles, and Scandinavian fiddle styles, and Scottish. Not so much Irish because it wasn't so easy to pick up. There's so many things on that wavelength. There's not a big scene up there for that type of music on television, fiddle music, but there were some really healthy radio programs going. You'd just tune in and listen to some tunes.

Jennifer: We used to listen to the shortwave radio from America. Hazel plays guitar in a very jazzy swing type style, which she got from a guy from Shetland called Peerie Willie Johnson. He's a really well-known guitar player. He recorded for years with Aly Bain and Violet Tulloch. He's about seventy-six now, but back in the '40s, when he was learning guitar, he used to listen to the shortwave radio from America, and the kind of thing they were playing was the Hot Club of France, Django Reinhardt, that kind of thing. So he used that sound and started applying it to traditional tunes. And I think, because of that American, Texan type of thing that he was getting, he started learning ragtime tunes, and things that were a bit jazzy. Everybody up there, I would say they probably play more ragtime and American style music than they do Irish, because Irish was never really a big inspiration, other than the obvious ones, like the Bothy Band, and Sean McGuire and people like that. But really, it wasn't as big an inspiration as it would be for probably the rest of Scotland or England.

Hazel: There was a junior Strathspey and Reel Society which went on for an hour before the actual Strathspey and Reel Society started at eight o'clock. We had one of the younger teachers there, a teenaged fiddle player, who would teach some of the really little kids between seven and eight o'clock. That was an opportunity for them — it's like a youth club for them, you know, their parents went and left them there and they could all run around screaming, buy their sweeties, their candy, and juice and things, and they'd just go crazy. And that was good because it was something that was fun that they could do on a weeknight, after school, and meet with all their friends, just like a youth club, or a sports club or something. Jenny and I taught that for about five years, I think.

Jennifer: Eventually, after we got to the seniors, we ended up being asked to do the juniors! It was good fun.

How would you characterize the main difference between Orkney style and Shetland styles?

Jennifer: I'd say the Shetland style, if you could take it down to its roots, they do actually have Shetland tunes that sound like you could play them on the Hardanger fiddle — they sound Scandinavian, Norwegian. Of course, we don't have that in Orkney. What we have is a lot more touch of Scottish, I would say, which is a lot more marches and strathspeys and things like that... And a lot of people say that the Orkney style is a bit more like it rolls along, which is very similar to Shetland music. Imagine Norwegian music, you don't really tap your feet to it and bob your head, because it's quite an unusual rhythm, and it sort of pushes and pulls all the time — Orkney music does that quite a lot. But the main difference is more influence from Scotland — it's not quite as ancient as Shetland.

Did you learn to read music in school?

Jennifer: I did, because I was always getting fiddle lessons and I studied classical for a long time as well… It was funny when we were in the Strathspey and Reel. All the old men, none of them read music at all — they all just played the tunes off the top of their head. And I was always so embarrassed because I had music with me. And so eventually I stopped. I started "forgetting" my music, on purpose, and my mom was saying, "You've forgotten your music!" And I said, "Oh, never mind, I'll take it next week." And I would go in and sit, and pretend to be playing without the music, and of course, eventually you manage to start picking up the tunes! But it was very strange, because all the old men were all dying to know how to read music, and I was wanting to play like them, without the music! It was a really funny contrast of the two ways. But reading music is a handy thing to be able to do, especially if you want to teach in a school.

Do you have any tips for beginning fiddlers?

Jennifer: Just stick at it, I suppose. It's very disheartening to start with. It sounds so awful to start with! But it does get better. Work at tapping your feet when you're playing — that helps you to keep your rhythm, because a lot of people suffer from speeding up and slowing down, especially if you play on your own. Tap your feet, and give every note its full value, don't cut it too short.

Hazel: It's really a good idea to practice with somebody. Or if you don't have anyone to play with, play along to a tape or a CD or a metronome. Timing is so important. And the other thing is, if you're an adult and you're learning any instrument, you should always try to totally open your mind. Imagine that you're a child. Children find it much easier to learn, because if you show them something, you say, "Do this," and they'll do it, and they don't say, "Why am I doing this?" or "That sounds horrible, I can't bear to listen to that," which an adult would do…Don't try to get everything perfect every time.

Jennifer: And don't hope to be a Johnny Cunningham in five minutes, because it will just destroy your ambitions really quickly!

[The Wrigleys' recordings, including their latest release, *Huldreland* (Greentrax Records, 1997), may be ordered from: Fiddlers Crossing, (626) 792-6323; fiddlers@earthlink.net; Tayberry Music, (803) 366-9739; mtice@cetlink.net; Ossian USA, (603) 783-4383; ossianusa@aol.com; Ossian Publications, P.O. Box 84, Cork City, Ireland; ossian@iol.ie. For bookings, contact the Stoneyport Agency, 39 Shandon Crescent, Edinburgh EH11 1QF, Scotland, (011 44) 131 346 8237; fax: (011) 131 313 2083; email: jb@folkmus.demon.co.uk]

Miss Sarah MacFayden

By Jennifer Wrigley. Transcribed by Donna Maurer as played by Jennifer and Hazel Wrigley on *The Watch Stone* (Attic Records 1994, ATCD038).

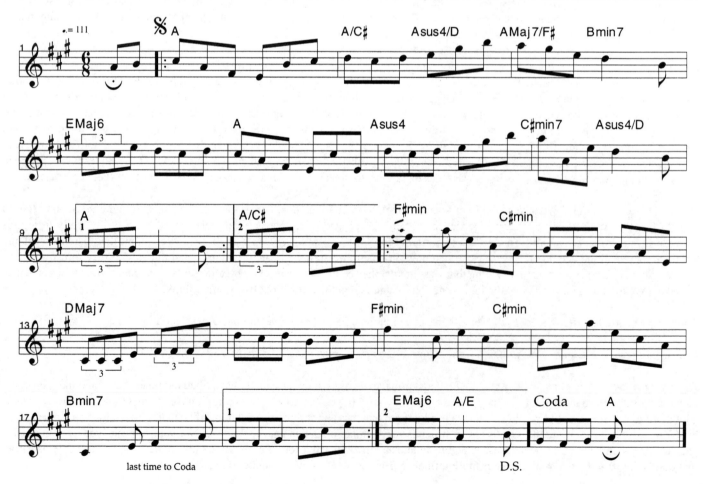

Kentucky Fiddle Music
— for Bruce Greene

They're out there, fiddlers
like Salyer, Hawkins, Fulks,
Phelps — the fiddling
descendants of fiddling
great-uncles, grandpas,
grannies — fiddling tunes
mournful and disturbing
as that late May frost
twenty-one years back
that ruined poplar
roots. The bowing dies
unless it's passed.
So you learn.

But what of those
you missed: Boley Tolan
of Vortex, Ida Stout
from near Eighty-Eight,
1st Sergeant Phineas Owens
of Shoulderblade, and so on —
their fiddling silenced.
And what of the ones
those you missed
would have pointed.
The journey to source
is an endless drive
into hollows and hills.

By Ken Waldman

[First published in *Sou'wester* (Southern Illinois University-Edwardsville). Reprinted with permission of the author, from *Fiddle Tunes: Old-Time Music Poems, Alaska-style.* Available from the Nomadic Press, 3705 Arctic, #1551, Anchorage, AK 99503 for $7 + $2 s/h.]

Jonathan

His work calloused hands accustomed
To the shape of wrenches and cows,
Now caress his violin
And fiddle music fills his house.

Weary from work in the barn and dairy,
The milky smell of hay and cattle.
With a gleam in his eye he forgets farming,
And patiently tunes the fiddle.

Sometimes he plays to amuse himself,
Or to entertain the neighbors.
They dance in his house of wide board floors,
He fiddles away his labors.

Some folks sing or play for glory,
Some folks sing for sorrow.
But this chap plays for pleasure only
Which gives him strength for tomorrow.

By Dudley Laufman

[From a pamphlet called "I Hear Ringing Reels," by Dudley Laufman. For information on Dudley's many books and recordings, contact him at P.O. Box 61, Canterbury, NH 03224, (603) 783-4719.]

Photo Credits

p. 13   Randal Bays; *photo by Rosalie Borda*
p. 19   Kevin Burke; *photo by Owen Carey*
p. 26   Michael Doucer; *photo by Robley Dupleix*
p. 45   John Hartford's; *photo by David Schenk*
p. 51   Jerry Holland; *photo by Carol Kennedy*
p. 55   Olov Johansson; *photo by Thomas Fahlander*
p. 62   Barbara Lamb; *photo by Benham Studios*
p. 65   Laurie Lewis; *photo by Anne Hamersky*
p. 68   Sandy MacIntyre; *photo by Claire McGuirk*
p. 71   Natalie MacMaster; *photo by KOCH*
p. 73   Frankie McWhorter; *photo by Mike Calcote*
p. 79   Jaun Reynoso; *photo by Tomás Casademunt, courtesy Discos Corason*
p. 82   Dale Russ; *photo by John Gallagher*
p.90   Björn Ståbi; *photo by Thomas Fahlander*
p. 93   Alicia Svigals; *photo by Helma Vincue ©1996*
p. 96   Athena Tergis and Laura Risk; *photo by Christine Alicino*
p. 99   Jay Ungar and Molly Mason; *photo by Michael Weisbrot*
p. 105   Claude "Fiddler" Williams; *photo by Wojtek Kubik ©1998*
p. 112   Jennifer and Hazel Wrigley; *photo by Norman Chalmers*

If you're enjoying this book, you're sure to love *Fiddler Magazine* — the quarterly for fiddlers of all levels and styles!

- 60+ pages per quarterly issue
- Feature articles on various regions and styles of fiddle playing written by experts in the field
- Interviews with top fiddlers
- Transcriptions of tunes (several per issue)
- Regular Columns: The Practicing Fiddler, Bluegrass Fiddling, Old Time Tunes, On Improvisation, The Irish Fiddler, Fiddle Care, Violin Makers, Reviews of books, recordings, videos
- And more!

What the Readers Say:

Thanks again for a wonderful publication. I'm not sure I could live without it (seriously!). — *Subscriber, Oregon*

…Page for page, I think *Fiddler Magazine* is one of the best music magazines — no, just one of the best magazines, period — that is published today. — *Subscriber, California*

Thank you for producing a truly inspiring magazine. Every issue contains some musical treasure… — *Subscriber, England*

What a great privilege to read your magazine and learn about the heritage of folk music from around the world. Thanks for providing a great learning tool… — *Subscriber, South Carolina*

Each issue is like a week at fiddle camp.
— *G. Fisch, Lake Emma Fiddle Camp, Saskatchewan*